A SELECTION

OF

ENGLISH SYNONYMS.

FIRST AMERICAN EDITION,

FROM THE SECOND LONDON EDITION,

REVISED AND ENLARGED.

BOSTON AND CAMBRIDGE:

JAMES MUNROE AND COMPANY.

MDCCCLII.

STEREOTYPE EDITION.

THURSTON, TORRY, AND EMERSON, PRINTERS.

EDITOR'S PREFACE.

THIS little work has been carefully revised by me, throughout; and though I am far from presuming to call it perfect, it is, I am confident, very much the best that has appeared on the subject.

Of the importance of that subject itself, very different opinions will probably be found to exist. Some advantage, indeed, all will acknowledge, in the cultivation of correctness and precision in our expressions. But the importance of this, and of all that relates to language, will be much less highly estimated by those who have adopted the metaphysical theory of *ideas*, and who consider the use of language to be merely the *conveying* our meaning to *others*, than by those who adhere to the opposite—the *nominalist*—view, (which I have set forth in the Introduction to the *Logic*, § 8,) and who accordingly regard words—or some kind of *signs* equivalent to words—as an indispensable instrument of thought, in all cases, where a process of *reasoning* takes place.

RICHARD DUBLIN.

PREFACE, BY THE AUTHOR.

In offering a collection of synonyms to the public, a few words of explanation may be necessary.

It is scarcely needful to remind the reader that the word 'synonym' is, in fact, a misnomer, as applied to words of the description in question. Literally, it implies an exact coincidence of meaning in two or more words: in which case there would be no room for discussion; but it is generally applied to words which would be more correctly termed *pseudo*-synonyms—*i. e.*, words having a shade of difference, yet with a sufficient resemblance of meaning to make them liable to be confounded together. And it is in the number and variety of these that (as the Abbé Girard well remarks) the richness of a language consists. To have two or more words with exactly the same sense, is no proof of copiousness, but simply an inconvenience. A house would not be called well furnished from its having a much larger number of chairs and tables of one kind than were needed, but from its having a separate article for each distinct use. The more power we have of discriminating the nicer shades of meaning, the greater facility we possess of giving force and precision to our expressions. Our own language possesses great advantages in this respect; for being partly derived from the Teutonic, and partly from the Latin, we have a large number of duplicates from the two sources; which are, for the most part, though not universally, slightly varied in their meaning.

These slight variations of meaning add to the copiousness of the English language, by affording words of more and less familiarity, and of greater and less force. This may be easily understood, if we consider that the branch of the Teutonic, spoken in England during the Anglo-Saxon period, never became extinct, but that three-fourths of the English language at present consist of words altered or derived from that ancient dialect; that these words usually express the most familiar ideas, such as *man*, *house*, *land*, &c.; and that the French terms gradually introduced, being those of a more highly civilized people, were adapted to express the more refined ideas. This is true even of physical objects; thus, for instance, most of the names of the animals used for food are still Teutonic, such as *ox*, *sheep*, *swine*, &c. The Anglo-Saxons, like the modern

Germans, had no objection to say *ox-flesh*, *sheep-flesh*, *swine's-flesh*,—but the Norman conquerors, introducing a more refined cookery, introduced with it French words for the flesh of the animal; hence we have *beef*, *mutton*, *pork*.*

We have entirely lost such compounds as *ox-flesh*, *sheep-flesh*, but we still retain *swine's-flesh*, with a peculiar modification of meaning, when we speak of it as one of the meats prohibited † by the Mosaic Law, in which case it is plain that it presents to the mind a gross idea, which *pork* does not.

In the case of such duplicates as have no assignable difference, it may happen, from the mere fact of the greater or less familiarity which one word presents to the mind, that although it be in most cases indifferent which we use, yet in some instances custom, founded on the facts above mentioned, makes a difference in their employment. (See the articles 'Liberty, Freedom,' 'Righteous, Just,' &c.)

It has not been the design of this work to notice *all* the synonyms in our language; which would, indeed, be an almost endless task; but merely (after excluding technical terms, and words which *do* exactly coincide) to select a few of those groups

---

* See the amusing remarks on this subject in the second chapter of Scott's *Ivanhoe*.

† Isai. lxv. 4; lxvi. 17. 2 Mac. vi. 18.

of words which are in most frequent use, and are most liable to be confounded.

Many persons imagine that two words must either coincide precisely in their meaning, so as to be, in the primary and strict sense of the word, 'synonymous,' or else stand for two (more or less) distinct *things*. Indeed, it would often be regarded as almost a truism to assert this; but those who maintain such an opinion overlook the fact, that two words, without exactly coinciding in sense, may nevertheless relate to one and the same thing, regarded in *two different points of view*. An illustration of this is afforded in the relation which exists between the words 'inference' and 'proof.' Whoever justly infers, proves; and whoever proves, infers: but the word 'inference' leads the mind from the premises which have been assumed, to the conclusion which follows from them: while the word 'proof' follows a reverse process, and leads the mind from the conclusion to the premises. We say, 'What do you infer *from* this?' and 'how do you *prove* that?'* Another illustration may be quoted in the synonyms 'expense' and 'cost'—considered elsewhere more at length. The same article may be expensive and

* See Whately's *Logic*, book IV. chap. iii. § 1, in which the above is illustrated by the difference between the road from London to York, and the road from York to London.

costly; but we speak of *expense* in reference to the means of the purchaser; of *cost*, in reference to the actual value of the article.

We have seldom in the following pages introduced, — what are usually considered so closely connected with the subject of synonyms as to demand a prominent place in a work of this kind, — namely, etymologies; which are generally appended to every group of synonyms as an almost essential part of it.

But it may be doubted whether this procedure does not tend to confuse the subject it was intended to clear. The history of the *derivation* of words is, indeed, one which offers a most interesting and important field of inquiry, and one which may accidentally throw light on their meanings; but the two questions are in themselves completely distinct; and, in inquiring into the actual and *present* meaning of a word, the consideration of what it *originally* meant may frequently tend to lead us astray.*

* The following notice is extracted from the Common-place Book of the late Bishop Copleston: —

'Words apparently synonymous — and really so in the great majority of instances — have nevertheless each an appropriate meaning, which on certain occasions is made to appear. The propriety of meaning is known, *à priori*, by the scholar who is acquainted with the etymology of the word, but the person who has collected its meaning only from its use is ever liable to mistakes, and often to

It is curious, and illustrative of national character and customs, to observe how completely words, radically the same, modify their meaning in the various languages which branch out from one common source. Who would expect to see words, so nearly the same, differ so widely in meaning as our English word altered (changed), the French 'alteré,' (overheated or thirsty,*) and the Italian 'alterato' (angry): and then, again, our English word *alternative*, (a choice between two courses,) and the Spanish 'alternativa,' (the social circle in which a person moves,) all these different words springing from the Latin 'alter' (another)? Who would suppose that the same word, the French 'défendre,' should signify 'to defend' and 'to forbid?' or that

---

the most ridiculous mistakes; because, perhaps, in the course of his experience, it has never been used in such a manner as to demonstrate its peculiar signification. *E. g.*, Benevolence and Philanthropy are frequently synonymous — they might, nine times out of ten, be substituted for one another; and an illiterate person, recollecting that each term is applied to characters and actions of kindness, mercy, and humanity, will indiscriminately use them, even when that humanity is shown towards the brute creation, than which mistake nothing could be more ludicrous.'

Many other words, however, are now used habitually with impropriety, as far as regards etymology, — as wine, tea, coffee, which originally signified liquors drawn from particular plants, and are now applied to any imitations of these liquors, as 'sage-tea,' 'ginger-wine.'

* It originally meant, altered *for the worse* — then, angry or excited — thence, heated, and, lastly, thirsty.

one word, honesty, (honnêteté,) should imply civility in France, and probity in England; and another, (virtus,) valor in Latin, and excellence in the arts in Italian? or that the three words 'substantia,' 'understanding,'* 'hypostasis,' should all three have corresponding origins, though so widely different in their signification?

Again, it is curious to observe what different ideas originally suggested the words which now mean precisely the same thing in different languages. The word 'Heaven,' for instance, conveyed with it the idea of something *heaved* or *lifted* up, as also the old word '*lift*,' and the German '*luft*.' 'Cœlum,' again, referred to something hollowed out or vaulted, being derived from the Greek word *koilon*, hollow, our own word 'coiled' being probably of the same origin. 'A torrent,' again, signified in Latin a stream, which was *burnt* up in summer, while the Greek word referred to its flowing (only) in winter.

All these variations of meaning help to elucidate national manners and habits of thought, and as such are valuable and curious; but though they may occasionally help us, they must not be allowed

---

* *Understanding* ('onderstonding') in Dutch, is *help*. 'Give me understanding that I may keep thy law' — would to a person comparing Dutch (as a cognate dialect) suggest, 'Give me help.'

to influence our decisions with respect to the significations of words. Our question is, not what *ought* to be, or formerly was, the meaning of a word, but what it *now* is; nor can we be completely guided by quotations from Shakspeare or Milton, or even from Addison or Johnson. Language has undergone such changes, even within the last sixty or seventy years, that many words, at that time considered pure, are now obsolete; while others (of which the word 'mob' is a specimen,)* formerly slang, are now used by our best writers, and received, like pardoned outlaws, into the body of respectable citizens. The standard we shall refer to in the present work, is the sense in which a word is used by the purest writers and most correct speakers of our own days.

A few observations may be added on the subject of conjugate or paronymous words; by which is meant, correctly speaking, different parts of speech from the same root, which exactly correspond in point of meaning: for example, the adjective 'expensive' is conjugate or paronymous with the substantive 'expense;' the verb 'to restrain' with the substantive 'restraint,' &c.

---

* The word 'flimsy' affords another instance of a word which was formerly a slang expression; it was a corruption of *film-sy*. It would not be found in Johnson's *Dictionary*.

But, like the word 'synonym,' this designation has been somewhat corrupted in its use; words being called 'conjugate,' which are in fact *pseudo*-conjugate — *i. e.*, which coincide in point of grammar and derivation, but not precisely in meaning. Such are 'sorrow' and 'sorry,' 'fright' and 'frightful,' and many others.

Where the conjugates exactly and completely correspond, we have sometimes used them indifferently in this work, as in the instance of 'expense' and 'cost,' answering respectively to 'expensive' and 'costly;' but where there is a shade of difference, it has been noticed, as being an important branch of the subject.

In order to avoid confusion, we have thought it best to divide the groups of synonyms according to the parts of speech — viz., into particles, nouns, adjectives, and verbs.

TABLE OF CONTENTS.

ADVERBS, PRONOUNS, PARTICLES.

VERBS.

ADJECTIVES.

NOUNS.

SYNONYMS.

ADVERBS, PRONOUNS, AND PARTICLES.

WHICH, THAT.

'WHICH' and 'that' are very often used synonymously; but there are some cases where either particle might be used, but where the sense of the whole would be materially altered by the choice made.

1st. 'Which' is used in speaking of a *class generally*, and 'that' when we mean to designate any particular *individual* of that class. For instance, in this sentence: 'A person who declines investing his money in a railway speculation *which* is highly advantageous,' we should imply that a railway speculation in general is an advantageous thing; but if we say, 'in a railway speculation *that* is highly advantageous,' we mean that *the particular speculation we are speaking of* is so. Again: 'The South-American Indians make great use of horses, which are very serviceable animals.' 'Which,' here implies that we are speaking of the *class* horse; if we said 'that,' it would seem to allude to some individual horses.

2dly, (and, indeed, this second rule follows from the first). 'That' is applied to the antecedent *immediately* preceding the relative, and 'which' to an antecedent sentence or part of a sentence. For instance: 'I should be unwilling at this juncture to introduce a new question *which* might raise objections.' This would imply that the introduction of any question might raise objections, whatever its purport might be; if we said '*that* might raise objections,' it would imply that this *individual question* itself might raise them.

IN SPITE OF, NOTWITHSTANDING.

'Notwithstanding' is a milder expression than 'in spite of.' 'In spite of' implies some decided obstacles to be overcome. 'Notwithstanding' simply indicates the presence of some circumstance which may be *supposed* to be an impediment. If we say, '*Notwithstanding* his youth, he has made great progress in his studies,' this would generally imply that the tender age which *might* have been an impediment to him, did *not* prove to be one; but when we say, '*In spite of* a bad education, his attainments are of a very high order,' we point out that the bad education *was* a real obstacle and impediment, which he was able to break through and overcome, but which could not be regarded as otherwise than an impediment. They are, however, often used synonymously; but 'notwithstanding' generally applies more to negative hinderances, passive difficulties; and 'in spite of' to active opposition. We should say, 'He was dragged along *in spite of* his resistance,' rather than 'notwithstanding.' Again, it would be a more polite form of expression to say, '*Notwithstanding* what you have said, I still think,' than '*In spite of* what you have said.'

To act *in spite of* experience, is to go against the lesson it teaches. But if we were to say, '*Notwithstanding* his experience, he acted thus,' we should imply that the person alluded to had *not* gained any such lessons by his experience.

WHILE, THOUGH.

'Though' implies more of *contrast* in the parallels made than 'while.' For instance, we should say, '*While* I admire his courage, I esteem his mildness and moderation;' but '*Though* I admire his courage, I detest his ferocity.' 'While' might be used, indeed, in both these cases, but 'though' necessarily implies contrast.

NEARLY, ALMOST.

These words are often used synonymously, but there is a slight difference between them: 'nearly' is applied rather to questions of quantity, time, and space: as, 'It is *nearly* eight o'clock'—'This child is *nearly* ten years old'—'I walked *nearly* two miles.' 'Almost' *might* be used in the same way, but it is less frequently so employed, and more commonly appropriated to questions of *degree;* as, for instance, 'It is *almost* as white as snow'—'He is so plain as to be *almost* ugly.' In this sense we should not say 'nearly.' 'Almost' is never used with a negative. We should say, 'She is not *nearly* so handsome as her sister;' in this case, 'almost' could not be applied.

COMPLETELY, ENTIRELY. SCARCELY, HARDLY.

These two pairs of adverbs bear very much the same relation to each other as 'nearly' and 'almost.' 'Completely,' like 'almost,' is used in questions of degree; 'entirely' in those of quantity. They are often used synonymously, but still we should say, 'I am *completely* tired,' not 'I am *entirely* tired,' and 'The space was *completely* (not entirely) filled up.' 'Scarcely,' again, relates to quantity; 'hardly' to degree. We say, 'He is *scarcely* ten years old,' 'it is *scarcely* a mile off;' but, 'I shall *hardly* be able to finish this work,' &c.

WITH, THROUGH, BY.

'By' and 'with' are in many cases used synonymously, but there are also many cases in which they convey a distinct meaning to the mind.

Whenever a certain effect is implied as proceeding from *two* causes, the remote and original cause is expressed by the use of 'by,' and the immediate one by 'with.' For instance: 'The tree was cut down *by* a woodman *with* an axe.' If we said '*by* an axe,' it would imply some free agency on the part of the axe. '*With* a woodsman,' on the other hand, would imply that the woodsman was an unconscious instrument in the tree's destruction. On the other hand, whenever a conscious agent is implied, we use the word 'by.'

This was not the case in old English: Shakspeare uses the expression — 'marred *with* traitors' — in modern speech it would be '*by* traitors' — but marred *with* the swords of traitors or *with* the wounds inflicted by them. In general, 'with' is improper, not only when a conscious agent is supposed, but when the agent is personified to a certain degree in our own minds, from its action being *apparently* voluntary. For instance, we hardly ever say 'struck *with* lightning' or '*with* a thunderbolt,' but '*by*:' although if another agency were poetically or mythically introduced, the expression would again be changed to 'with,' as 'Jupiter struck him to the ground *with* a thunderbolt.'

'By' and 'with' are often used when no agent is spoken of, but a certain object is said to be accomplished by *certain means*. But in this case, 'by' implies that the means used are essential; 'with,' only that they are useful in aiding our endeavors. The two following phrases, '*By* patience and perseverance the work will be completed,' or '*with* patience,' &c., would be equally correct: but the word 'by' implies that patience and perseverance are the chief instruments in accomplishing the work; while 'with' points out merely that they will prove useful auxiliaries in its prosecution.

'By' and 'with,' however, have each separate meanings of their own, completely distinct from those we have just mentioned, but tending to throw additional difficulty on the subject of their relation to each other. 'With' implies *companionship* as well as instrumentality; and 'by'—without reckoning the cases in which it is synonymous with 'beside'—is also applied to designate the *mode* of performing some act; as, 'this is locked *by* a key, tied *by* a string, shut *by* a clasp;' 'we travelled *by* railroad;' 'the letter was sent *by* express.' In Greek and Latin, 'with' was expressed by the dative or ablative case; 'by,' by the word 'hypo' in Greek, (with a genitive,) and *a* or *ab* in Latin (with an ablative.)

'Through' is somewhat different from the other words mentioned. It often implies that the means used are the *appointed channel* for the conveyance of the object or advantage specified; as 'I heard the news *through* such a person;' 'I received a remittance *through* the bank.'

BUT, HOWEVER, YET, STILL, NOTWITHSTANDING, NEVERTHELESS.

'But,' like its corresponding conjunctions in French, Italian, and Greek, has two distinct meanings, one in a certain sense conjunctive, and the other disjunctive. The one would be expressed at full length by 'but yet,' the other by 'but on the contrary.' For instance: 'This is not summer, *but* it is almost as warm,' would express the first, and 'This is not summer *but* winter,' the second. Horne Tooke was so struck with the difference of these two meanings of 'but,' that he referred the word to two separate roots, one being 'boot,' (besides,) the other '*be-out*,' (left out.) Ingenious as this theory is, it is hardly tenable; for not only in French and Italian, but even in Greek, there is but one conjunction to express these two different meanings.* In German, Spanish, and Latin, we find a conjunction for each of these two meanings; the German *aber*, the Spanish *pero*, the Latin *autem*, answering to 'but yet;' and *sondern*, *sino*, and *sed*, to 'but on the contrary.'

The other words in the group before us all correspond to the *first* of these two meanings ('but yet'). The weakest of them all in disjunctive power is 'however,' which seems rather to waive the question than to qualify or alter it. 'This, *however*, is not essential,' differs in force from, '*but* this is not essential;' the latter rather implying that it might be *thought* essential.

'Yet' is stronger than 'but,' and 'still' even stronger again, as it indicates an exception to what has been said before. It seems an abbreviation of 'not removed.' 'All you say is true, *still* I think'—this implies that full weight is given to the opponent's arguments, but that they do not remove the difficulty in the mind of the objector. 'Notwithstanding' and 'nevertheless' are, again, stronger than 'still.' 'Nevertheless' is strongest of all.

ALSO, TOO, LIKEWISE, BESIDES.

'Too' is a slighter, and a more familiar expression than

* 'Boot,' however, is probably the origin of 'but,' as 'allos,' (another,) is of 'alla,' (but,) in Greek. So in Latin 'cæterum' signifies 'but.' Horne Tooke may have intended to allude to a third sense of the word 'but,' where it bears the same meaning as 'except,' which does literally imply 'left out' And even this third meaning is probably derived from 'boot,' (first implying addition, and afterwards exception,) just as in old English we sometimes see the word 'beside' loosely used for 'except,' as 'all *beside* him.' The Greek *pleen*, except, was probably derived from *pleion*, more.

'also,' which has something in it more specified and formal. This is the only difference between the two words. 'Likewise' has a rather different meaning. Originally it meant, 'in like manner,' and it has preserved something of that signification. It implies some connection or agreement between the words it unites. We may say, 'He is a poet, and likewise a musician:' but we should not say, 'He is a *prince*, and likewise a musician,' because there is no natural connection between these qualities: but 'also' implies merely addition.

'Besides' is used rather when some additional circumstance is named *after* others; as a kind of after-thought, and generally to usher in some new clause of a sentence; as, '*Besides* what has been said, this must be considered,' &c.

VOLUNTARILY, WILLINGLY.

'Voluntarily' is more restricted in its sense than 'willingly;' it simply means that the thing done is not performed under immediate compulsion, nor without intention. All our outward actions are *voluntary*,—for that cannot be called an action which is not voluntary; but they are not necessarily performed *willingly;* for *this* implies that our wishes and inclinations go along with the action performed. There are many things which are done voluntarily, but are much against the wishes of the agent. For instance, in Roman-catholic countries a girl who takes the veil must do so *voluntarily;* but it frequently happens that she is far from doing it willingly; the entreaties and threats of her friends, unhappiness at home, despair of a better fate, will often induce her to *decide* on taking a step which nevertheless is quite against her inclination. Originally, however, these words, 'willingly' and 'voluntarily,' must have had the same meaning.

THEREFORE, WHEREFORE, THEN, ACCORDINGLY, HENCE, THENCE, SO, CONSEQUENTLY.

All these are what are called *illative* particles — *i. e.*, particles which denote that which in some way follows from what has been previously said; but they denote this in different ways.

'Therefore' and 'wherefore' are nearly alike, but 'therefore' may indicate a conclusion from several reasons adduced; 'wherefore' refers only to something immediately preceding. We might say — 'This and that and the other difficulty will attend such a procedure; I cannot, *therefore*, approve of this measure.' And again: 'I found his testimonials insufficient, *wherefore* I refused to appoint him.' 'Wherefore' is, however, rather obsolete. In old English, it was used to signify not only 'for which cause,' but also 'for what cause;' as 'the more part knew not *wherefore* they were gathered together.' (Acts, xx. 32.)

'Then' bears the same relation to 'therefore' that 'as' does to 'because;' it is less formally conclusive, and is used more by the way and incidentally than 'therefore.' Whenever the *main object* is to establish a certain proposition, the word 'therefore' is used; when this point is subsidiary, 'then' is to be preferred. In establishing a proposition of Euclid, it would be inappropriate to say, 'the angles of a triangle are *then* equal,' &c.: 'therefore' would be the proper word. In using 'then,' we often imply that the proposition on which our argument is based is taken for granted; it seems to say, 'Recollect this has been proved.'

In old English, 'therefore' is used where 'then' is now; as '*Therefore* being justified by faith, we have peace,' &c., we should now say, 'Being then justified by faith,' as the question had been already discussed and fully established. 'Hence' and 'thence' resemble 'then' more than 'therefore;' they answer nearly to 'this' and 'that,' the one indicating an antecedent reason close at hand; the other, one more remote.

'Accordingly' is something like 'therefore,' but more limited in its meaning. 'Therefore' includes both inference and proof* — both physical and logical sequence; 'accordingly,' only the former. We might say, 'It has rained, *therefore* — or *accordingly* — the ground is wet;' and 'It is wet, *therefore* it has rained:' in this last sense we could not use 'accordingly.' 'Therefore,' 'accordingly,' and 'then,' often indicate a practical course of action following from certain causes or reasons; 'hence' and 'thence' are applied exclusively to reasoning. For instance, 'I determined not to act hastily, and *therefore* consulted the best advisers. Such an one's opinion seemed to me the most just, and *accordingly* I adopted the course of action he recommended; I fixed *then* upon this plan,' &c. In such a sentence, 'hence' and 'thence' could not be used; but we say, '*hence* we may infer,' or '*thence* we may conclude.'

'So' is something like 'then,' but slighter and more colloquial.

'Consequently' is the most formally and deliberately conclusive of the whole group; it is generally confined to a *practical* sequence or conclusion, and is seldom used in mere speculative argument.

BECAUSE, SINCE, INASMUCH AS, FOR, AS.

These are all causal particles; *i. e.*, they indicate a proposition *from* which something follows; they correspond, *conversely*, to the illative, which point out that which *does* follow.

'Because' (by cause) would seem from its etymology to

---

* See Whately's *Logic* — Inference and Proof.

have originally referred only to physical sequence, but is now used as an answer to 'why?' in the three senses in which it may be asked, 1st, indicating *physical* sequence, (from what cause?) as, 'Why are the days longest in summer?' 2dly, *logical* sequence, (how is it proved?) as, 'Why is this line equal to that?' and 3dly, 'For what purpose?' as, 'Why did you go to London yesterday?'

'Since' is more incidental and less formal than 'because;' it also generally begins the sentence, or is understood as the beginning.

'Inasmuch as' has something of a qualifying power, which the others do not possess; it is nearly the same as 'in as far.' This sentence, for example,—'I approve of his sentiments, *inasmuch* as they are patriotic,' would imply that they are approved *only* so far and no further. If we substituted 'because,' we should be accounting for, instead of qualifying, our approbation.

'As' is even more incidental than 'since,' and seems to take for granted what is stated; for instance, in saying, '*As* I know him to be dishonest, I must take these precautions'—the fact of the dishonesty is merely noticed in passing, as something already established; just as in the relation of 'then' to 'therefore.' 'As' seems to suppose its corresponding word 'so' to follow. In our earlier writers 'so' is generally expressed; but unless some very strict comparison is intended, it is commonly omitted by moderns.*

'For' is a slighter 'because.' In the older writers, as Shakspeare, we may find it used as 'because' would be now: 'I hate him for he is a Christian.'—(*Merchant of*

* Thus in a letter of Sir F. Walsingham to Harleigh: 'As your studie in these things is very commendable, so I thank you for the same;' in modern language this would be, 'as your studie, &c., I thank you.'

Venice). Cowper has accordingly introduced it into *John Gilpin*, which is an imitation of the antique style, 'for that wine is dear,' &c.

AMID, AMIDST, AMONG, AMONGST.

These words preserve much of their etymological signification. 'Among' originally signified 'one out of many': 'amid' and 'amidst,' 'in the middle of.' Hence, then, 'among' and 'amongst' always imply *number*, 'amid' and 'amidst' generally *quantity*. We should say,—'*Among*' (not 'amidst') 'all these books I cannot find the one I want;' but not, 'I was out *among* snow and rain:' in this last case 'amidst' would be the correct expression.

'Amid' and 'amidst' also indicate that the thing specified is of a different class from those around it; while 'among' and 'amongst' are oftener (though not always) applied to objects surrounded with those of the same class. We speak of 'a rose *amidst* nettles,' but not of 'a tree *amidst* the forest;' we are said to be '*among* friends,' but '*amidst* enemies.' *

BETWIXT, BETWEEN.

'Betwixt' is ordinarily confined to places; 'between' has

---

* In poetry these rules are not strictly adhered to. See Milton's description of the seraph Abdiel:—

> 'faithful found,
> *Among* the faithless faithful only he:
> Among innumerable false, unmov'd,
> Unshaken, unseduced, unterrified,
> His loyalty he kept, his love, his zeal:
> Nor number, nor example, with him wrought
> To swerve from truth, or change his constant mind
> Though single. From *amidst* them forth he pass'd.'
>
> *Paradise Lost*, Book V.

Here the two words are used indifferently.

a much more extended signification. We speak of—'what may happen *between* morning and evening,' of 'hesitating *between* opposite courses:' we could not use 'betwixt' in these senses; but '*betwixt* the chair and the table,' '*betwixt* the road and the mountain,' would be quite correct. In poetry, however, 'betwixt' is used much as 'between' is in prose: as in Scott's ballad of 'Alice Brand,'—'*Betwixt* night and day,' &c.

THOUGH, ALTHOUGH.

These particles nearly approach each other in meaning; but 'although' is the stronger and more emphatic of the two, and is therefore generally chosen to begin a sentence: as,—'*Although* my difficulties are great, I hope to succeed.' It seems to imply that full weight is allowed to the former clause of the sentence, and to answer to the additional 'all' so often introduced into old English, as, '*all* too soon,'* a combination still preserved in German,—'all zu-wohl,' or 'gar zu schön.'

INDEED, NAY.

'Indeed' still preserves its original etymological meaning, which is nearly the same as—'in reality,' 'in fact,' 'in truth.' When used synonymously with 'nay,' it generally adds to the force of the second clause of a sentence,—as, 'I know it, *indeed* I am sure of it.' 'Nay' has this force in a much more intense degree, and makes the second clause even stronger in proportion to the first than 'indeed,'—as, 'I think, *nay*, I am sure.' In old English, 'yea' had nearly the same sense as 'nay' has now,—as in Cor. ix., '*yea*, I judge not mine ownself:' in modern English the

---

* The particle 'alto,' likewise used in old English, and meaning 'entirely,' is sometimes confounded with this expression. But in 'all too soon,' 'entirely' could not have been meant.

word 'nay' would have been here employed. Each of them signifies, 'this is not all, *for* —;' or, 'not only this, *but* —.' These ellipses were often expressed in Greek by 'alla' (but) or 'gar' (for). An instance where this ellipse was mistaken by our translators occurs in 1 Cor. xv., —'*for* one star differeth from another in glory.' The Greek word used is the one usually translated 'for;' but 'nay,' or 'indeed,' would have been the correct rendering of the idea in English.

ONLY, SOLELY, ALONE, MERELY, SIMPLY.

'Only' (preserving its etymology, *one-ly*) relates to cases of number, time, or quantity, which none of the others do: as, 'I have *only* one left;' 'he *only* left me just now.'

But when 'only' relates to questions *unconnected* with time, number, or quantity, 'solely' approaches the nearest to it in sense. It differs, however, in being more emphatic and deliberate, and in marking more distinctly the exception indicated. For instance, the phrase, 'I resolved to attend *only* to this case,' draws the attention to the abandonment of all others; while 'I attended *solely* to this,' points out the circumstance of one being singled from the rest. Or we might say, 'This I have mentioned is *only* one out of many reasons;' but, 'I have been influenced *solely* by this consideration.' In the former sentence the word 'only' could not be substituted. 'Alone,' when used as a particle, has nearly the same meaning as 'only.'

'Merely' and 'simply' somewhat resemble each other; but 'merely' conveys (at present) the sense of 'no more than;' while 'simply' seems (according to its original meaning) to convey a disavowal of complex acts or motives in the speaker. The *former* implies no *addition* — the *latter*, no *admixture*. For instance, 'this is *merely* a personal argument,' implies that nothing *more* is urged: 'this is *simply* a statement of facts,' excludes the idea of any comment accompanying it.

'Only' might be used for any of the other three particles.*

EXCEPT, EXCEPTING, BUT, SAVE.

'Except' and 'excepting' are nearly the same, the latter being more cumbrous and less in use.

The chief difference between them and 'but' is, that 'except' seems to imply a more decided and emphatic exclusion of the case specified than 'but.' 'I have written all my letters *but* one,' conveys a less marked exception than 'all *except* one.' 'Save' is almost exclusively limited to poetry.

---

* 'I *only* meant
To show the reed on which you leant,
Deeming this path you might pursue
Without a pass from Roderick Dhu.'

SCOTT'S *Lady of the Lake,* Canto V.

VERBS.

TO ALLOW, PERMIT, SUFFER, TOLERATE.

'To allow,' and 'to permit,' are often used synonymously; but 'to allow' is used rather more in the active,—'permit,' in the passive sense. In saying, 'I *allow* him to walk in my garden,' we seem to give a positive sanction to the action; 'I *permit* him,' simply implies that 'I do not hinder him.'

'To *suffer*' is more passive than either. It implies rather tolerance than sanction. An indolent and careless teacher will *suffer* his pupils to neglect their lessons; if we said, he *allowed* or *permitted* them, it would imply that he formally *gave them leave* to be idle. To *tolerate* is *always* used in the sense of permitting something unpleasant or otherwise objectionable to the tolerator; thus, we speak of *tolerating* differences in religion, &c.

TO CONFESS, ACKNOWLEDGE, OWN, AVOW.

'To confess' is to make a declaration of some action we have done, which is not known by the persons to whom we speak; as a Roman-catholic penitent *confesses* his sins to his priest. If the action is already known, but not the author of it, the declaring ourselves to be the doers of it would be called *acknowledging*, or *owning*. Or again, if *both* the action and the doer of it are known, we *acknowledge* it, by declaring our consciousness of it, as for instance, we *acknowledge* or *own* a fault which we are already known to have committed. Hence we speak of a person's 'refusing to *acknowledge* himself in the wrong,' which implies that his fault is already known; but we should speak of 'extorting a *confession*,' not 'an acknowledgment,' from a criminal; — because his confession would be a statement of facts not *supposed*, at least, to be known to others.

We sometimes speak of 'acknowledging' or 'confessing' — indifferently — some fault: but in using the word *confess* we are pointing out the fact that we are not known to be the doers of the action; while in using the word *acknowledge* we are rather adverting to the fact that the action itself is known. If both the action and the doer of it were known, we could not speak of 'confessing it.' We do indeed speak of '*confessing* our sins to God,' to whom all must be known; but this is rather said figuratively, — as we are commanded in the Scriptures 'to make our requests known' to Him, though of course they must be known already before we make them. But in both these cases the words used refer to our own state of mind.

Confessing is oftener applied in reference to a *fault* than either owning or acknowledging: indeed, strictly speaking, it almost always implies some error. 'To avow' is never used in the sense of *confessing a fault*, though the noun *avowal* sometimes is. But 'to avow' implies a bold, frank acknowledgment of the truth. We never *avow* what we are ashamed of; but we avow our motives, the reasons of our conduct, our opinions, &c. We *confess* our weakness, errors, or faults — we *acknowledge* or *own* what we are charged with.

The conjugate word 'confessor,'* is used in two senses, both very unlike those implied by the verb; first, indicating

---

* It is curious that this word and one other — *i. e.*, 'prisoner' — present almost the only exceptions to the general rule in our language, that the terminations 'or' and 'er' indicate an agent, and not a passive recipient.

one who *receives* a confession, and secondly, one who has boldly *avowed* his religious faith, (whether previously known or not,) and has suffered for that avowal. This last employment of the word probably grew out of the older and less defined use of the verb 'to confess,' which, as we may see in our translation of the Bible, was often formerly used where we should *now* substitute the word 'avow,' or 'acknowledge.'

TO CHARM, ENCHANT, ENRAPTURE, CAPTIVATE, FASCINATE, ATTRACT.

'To charm,' 'to enchant,' and 'to enrapture,' have a considerable resemblance in meaning. They differ chiefly in point of force; 'enchant' being stronger than 'charm,' and 'enrapture' stronger still. This last word is distinguished also from the other two, by implying a powerful excitement of *feeling*, as well as of taste or fancy; and by being very rarely, if ever, applied to the feelings awakened by *persons.*

'To attract' is to draw after one, — to win upon a person's liking, — to inspire an inclination. It is used generally for persons; whereas the other three terms apply equally well to things. We are charmed or enchanted with beautiful poetry, music, or scenery, by personal beauty or agreeable manners, — we are *attracted* by person and manners only. The conjugate word 'attraction' is less limited in specification; we speak of places, pursuits, &c., as having a 'strong *attraction.*'

'To captivate' and 'to fascinate' have nearly the same meaning as 'to attract;' but they are stronger terms, and the latter implies something of design; we use it in speaking of the manners of an accomplished woman of the world, who knows and uses her power. The conjugate adjective 'fascinating' does not convey so unfavorable a meaning, though it generally implies more of art than 'captivating' or 'attractive.'

TO CONTEMN OR SHOW CONTEMPT, DESPISE, SCORN, DISDAIN.

'To contemn' is less commonly used than its conjugate noun, *contempt*. This word is nearly the same in its meaning as 'to despise,' or rather it may be said that *despise* is the verb, and *contempt* the noun belonging to it. A proud man *despises* or feels *contempt* for those beneath him. Both imply looking down upon others, considering them as unworthy of notice. 'To contemn' is rather different in its meaning, both from 'to despise' and also from its own conjugate, 'contempt.' We never speak of *contemning* an *individual;* the expression is exclusively applied to qualities. We may despise, or feel contempt for persons who act in such or such a way; we only *contemn* their actions, or the dispositions which lead to those actions.

'To scorn' and 'to disdain' are used in a stronger sense than the words before mentioned. These verbs, like 'contemn,' are never properly used towards persons, though their conjugate nouns are. We are said to *treat* an inferior with scorn or disdain, but not to scorn or disdain him. Disdain implies a feeling of haughty *indignation*. The Italian *sdegno* is evidently from the same root, and somewhat resembles in its meaning our own word, though it is more frequently used to designate anger. *Disdain* is shown by a haughty supercilious manner, — *contempt* often shows itself in good-humored condescension. *Scorn* implies a mocking, scoffing spirit, — it forms a kind of link in its meaning between contempt and *ridicule*.

We have said that the verbs 'to scorn' and 'to disdain' are used rather towards things than persons. We speak of 'disdaining' or 'scorning' a proposal or course of action;

but there is a shade of differenee in the meaning. We disdain something which we consider beneath our station, capacity, or powers; we scorn what is *in itself* disgraceful or contemptible. Alexander *disdained* to share the Persian Empire with Darius, though it was a compromise very fitting for Parmenio: he would have *scorned* to do anything unworthy of a Macedonian.

TO CONQUER, SUBDUE, VANQUISH, SUBJUGATE.

'To conquer' is less individual and more general in its meaning than 'to vanquish:' we *vanquish* an enemy who attacks us; we *conquer* a country.

'Vanquish' is always used for a combat, generally with some *personal* enemy; 'conquer' for a series of combats. We speak of *vanquishing* an enemy in a single encounter, but of *conquering* a country. Achilles *vanquished* Hector before Troy; Napoleon, in his campaigns, *conquered* great part of Europe.

'To conquer' is oftener used metaphorically than 'to vanquish;' we talk of conquering evil inclinations, conquering oneself, &c. But in this last sense, 'to subdue' is oftener used. 'Subdue' implies a more continued pressure, and a more gradual, but surer and final victory.

When a nation has ceased to resist, we say it is subdued. 'Subjugate' (which originally means, to bring under the yoke) implies *external* and continued restrictions. We *subdued* the French, but we did not *subjugate* them. Poland is subjugated — that is to say, kept under by a continuous pressure from without; but its spirit remains unsubdued.

'Subjugate' is always used in speaking of *nations* — never of individuals, and never in an abstract sense. 'Subdue' may be applied to individuals even in a literal sense, but always indicates mental as well as physical conquest. A child, or a captive, is said to be completely *subdued* by severe treatment, when the spirit is broken and the mind enfeebled, or *cowed*, as it is sometimes expressed.

TO ASK, REQUEST, BEG, BESEECH, SUPPLICATE, ENTREAT, IMPLORE, SOLICIT.

'To ask' (not in the sense of inquiring) is the simplest form of making a request. 'Request' is merely a more polite form of asking. 'To beg' is stronger; a starving man is said to *beg*, not to *ask*, for alms.

'To beseech' is the same as to beg, but stronger still, and more high-flown and poetical. 'To entreat,' again, is nearly the same; but *beseeching* is more urgent — *entreating* more argumentative: we entreat an equal; we beseech a superior; we entreat a person on whom we are urging advice, when he is, in fact, receiving a favor from us: in this sense it is merely to urge strongly.

'To supplicate' and 'to implore' both imply extreme distress and urgency of entreaty; but we implore equals — we supplicate superiors. Supplication generally implies a state of humiliation and abject inferiority; a slave will supplicate pardon of his master — a captive supplicate a conqueror to spare his life. These two last verbs are stronger than any of the other mentioned. 'To solicit,' on the other hand, is simply to make a request to some one whom we address as our superior.

The government of these eight verbs is somewhat different. 'To ask,' 'to beg,' 'to request,' govern *commonly*, though not *always*, the *object sought;* the other five, generally the *person* to whom the request is made. We *ask* a *favor*, a mendicant begs his *bread;* but we implore or supplicate some one to grant us our request. This rule, however, does not universally hold good: we may ask a *person* for something, entreat a favor, implore pardon.

TO BEAR, SUFFER, ENDURE.

'To suffer,' when used as an *intransitive* verb, implies simply to be in pain or distress of body or mind. 'To bear' or 'endure,' is to support that distress with fortitude. It is true that the adverbs, 'patiently,' 'firmly,' 'resolutely,' are generally added to the verbs 'to bear' and 'to endure;' but still they have not so decidedly a *negative* action as 'to suffer:' we may say, 'He *suffers* a great deal, but has no idea of *bearing* pain'—'it is impossible to *bear* (or endure) such distress,' &c.; meaning, to bear with fortitude. 'Endure' is often used synonymously with 'bear,' but it generally implies bearing for a long continuance. 'To suffer,' when *transitively* used, is nearly the same as 'to tolerate.'

I have called the verb 'to suffer' an *in*transitive verb when applied to the endurance of pain or distress; for though it is true that we often speak of 'suffering pain,' &c., yet it seems to be rather an elliptical expression for 'suffering *under* or *from* pain,' as no action takes place; and we could not reverse the expression, and speak of pain 'being *suffered*,' though we often speak of its being *borne* or *endured*. This seems to show the intransitive character of the verb 'to suffer,' in the sense under consideration.

TO PUZZLE, PERPLEX, EMBARRASS.

We are *puzzled* when our intellectual faculties are confused, and we cannot comprehend what is proposed to us: we are *perplexed* when the feelings and will are brought into play as well as the intellect, and we are at a loss what to decide or how to act. We are *embarrassed* by some hinderance or difficulty which impedes our powers of thought, speech, or action. This need not necessarily be an intellectual hinderance; it is generally either of a kind which affects the feelings, as timidity or bashfulness, or a material obstacle which hampers us, such as an impediment in the speech. A schoolboy is *puzzled* with a difficult sum: a riddle puzzles those who try to guess it: we are *perplexed* by the subtleties of a casuist, or in the midst of conflicting opinions: a rustic is *embarrassed* in the presence of his superiors, or a traveller when trying to speak a foreign language he knows but imperfectly. It is the characteristic of embarrassment to take away our presence of mind.

The French use the word 'embarrass,' not only in our sense, but also as we should use the expression 'hampered' or encumbered. We use the word in this sense when we speak of 'embarrassed circumstances.'

TO FORBID, PROHIBIT.

The expression 'to prohibit' has more of an official character than is implied by 'to forbid,' which is oftener used in relation to private life. A government *prohibits* contraband goods: a schoolmaster *forbids* his pupils to break the rules of the school.

TO GUIDE, DIRECT, SWAY.

'To guide' and 'to direct' are words similar to the results which they indicate, but not similar in the means by which these results are attained. We may be *directed* from a distance: a *guide* must accompany and keep close to us.

A person in a road unknown to him requires directions. A blind man needs a guide. A general may direct the movements of his army from head-quarters: a ship is not directed, but guided, by the pilot or steersman. Directions are often nearly equivalent to commands, with this difference, that they always imply *instructions how* to act in some particular case, and not merely a positive order. We may command a person to be silent, or to speak: we could not, in such a case, be said 'to direct;' we direct a child or scholar to perform the prescribed task.

'To sway' implies a *propelling* force, which neither of the other words do, and also implies that the person who sways is *himself* the propelling force. It is most generally used in an abstract or moral sense, and in such cases, always indicates an exertion of the *lower* faculties. A man is guided or directed by his reason or intellect, but swayed by his passions or interests.

TO MISLEAD, DELUDE.

'To mislead' is, simply, to lead astray in any manner: 'to delude,' is to mislead by acting on the imagination. A man may be *misled* by any one who gives him bad advice; Mahomet *deluded* his followers with his visionary tales and pretended inspiration.

'To delude' always implies some *intention* to deceive; when we speak of being 'deluded by passion or vanity' we personify the qualities mentioned, and speak as if they were agents with evil intentions. 'To mislead' does not necessarily imply design: we may be misled by the obscurity of writing on a sign-post, or by a mistaken interpretation from a foreign language; the word *deluded* could not be used in such a case.

TO THINK, BELIEVE, SURMISE, SUPPOSE, PRESUME, CONJECTURE.

'To think,' is used in three senses.

1st. To express the ordinary operations of the intellect.

2d. An opinion formed in the mind; and,

3d. A belief in something as nearly, but not quite certain.

The threefollowing sentences are specimens: —

'*Thinking* is a useful exercise for the mind.'

'I *think* this a sensible book.'

'I *think* such and such an event has happened, but I am not sure.'

'To believe' has also two meanings; one, a decided *faith* in some opinion; the other, nearly synonymous with the third meaning of 'to think;' as, 'I *believe*, but am not sure,' which is nearly the same as 'I think,' but expresses a rather stronger conviction.

'To suppose' has also two senses; one in which we *assume* a thing for the sake of argument; the other, in which we conclude it to be most likely. 'We will *suppose* such a thing to be the case.' 'I *suppose* this must be true.'

'To presume' is to go upon a supposition, to consider the 'burden of proof' as on the other side. (See Whately's *Rhetoric.*) *Presumption* is not quite conjugate to the verb 'presume,' being weaker. 'There is a *presumption* in favor of his guilt, because he is a bankrupt,' is different from, 'We may *presume* he is guilty.' 'To conjecture' and 'to surmise,' with their respective substantives, which are strictly conjugate to the verbs, are nearly, but not quite alike. We *conjecture* in a case in which we have little or no direct evidence to go upon. 'To surmise' is nearly the same, but differs —

First, in being always *practical.* We may form *conjectures* about the volcanoes in the moon, or the immateriality of the soul: we can only *surmise* the truth of some practical transaction, as the reality of a crime being committed.

Secondly, a surmise is a *strong* conjecture, and must be founded on more evidence. We might say, 'I can form no *surmise* in a case like this, it must be a matter of mere *conjecture.*'

Thirdly, a surmise is always expressed and brought forward: a conjecture may be kept to ourselves; and, lastly, a surmise is generally unfavorable. We may *conjecture* the innocence of a suspected criminal: we *surmise* his guilt.

TO ABANDON, DESERT, FORSAKE.

We may *abandon* not only persons but things: we can only *desert* a person or a cause. A man abandons house, lands, and wealth; he deserts his friends, his country, or his standard.

'To abandon' is generally, though not always, blameable. It usually implies that the thing or person abandoned suffers some loss; hence, it must imply blame, except in an abstract case, such as 'abandoning a useless pursuit or hopeless undertaking.' 'To desert' is always disgraceful, even when used in an abstract sense. 'To desert' a cause, is to abandon it in a case where it cannot be abandoned without disgrace. A soldier who *abandons* his standard shamefully *deserts* his duty.

'Forsake' is rarely, if ever, used in reference to anything abstract: we may forsake a house, friends, or country; but not fortune, rank, or station. It is also distinguished from the other two words by implying no blame. An early Christian might forsake his family and friends for his religion: he would not be said to abandon them, except when reproached by his heathen enemies. It likewise implies no *loss* to the person or thing forsaken.

The conjugate particles are all more or less different: 'forsaken' is nearly the same as deserted, and both imply loss or bereavement; they in fact nearly correspond to the verb 'abandon.' To abandon a place is to leave it *deserted.*

TO ABDICATE, RESIGN, RELINQUISH.

We can only *abdicate* a high dignity or station; we may *resign* any situation, high or low — or indeed any advantage. A king abdicates his crown; a private person may resign wealth or station; a servant may resign his place: in short, any benefit may be resigned. 'To relinquish' is oftener used for *claims* of some kind — something whose possession is disputed or struggled for; as, for example, a contested inheritance. But it always implies yielding *after a struggle.* We might say, 'He would not *resign* his claims to the property without an effort; but after a long struggle, he was compelled to *relinquish* his object.'

TO DISTINGUISH, DISCRIMINATE.

'To distinguish' is merely to mark broad and obvious differences; 'to discriminate' is to notice minuter and more subtle differences. The generality of people can *distinguish* color; but many who possess the faculty to a certain point do not readily *discriminate* between the nicer shades. An ignorant man can distinguish a rose from a lily: only a botanist can discriminate between the varieties most closely allied and nearly resembling. The faculty of distinguishing belongs to every one whose intellect is above that of a child or a brute: it is only those who are skilled or well informed in any particular department who can discriminate clearly.

TO TEACH, INSTRUCT, INFORM, EDUCATE.

Of these words the first two are often used synonymously, but they have also a distinct meaning. 'Teaching,' strictly speaking, when distinguished from instruction, is applied to the practice of an art or branch of knowledge: instruction to the theory. A child is (correctly speaking) *instructed* in the grammar of a language, and *taught* to speak the language. Thus, teaching may be merely mechanical; while 'instruction' implies a degree of understanding in the pupil, as well as the master. A child who has been *taught* to learn lessons by rote, without understanding them, will find difficulty in comprehending *instruction* in the principles of what he has learned. Hence, we speak of *teaching* a brute, but never of *instructing* it.

Information,* again, is distinguished from instruction, in relation to the truths conveyed by it. Matters of fact, made known to one who could not have known them before, are called information: instruction elicits new truths out of subject-matter *already* existing in the mind. (See Whately's *Logic*, book iv. § 1.)

A traveller gives us information respecting foreign countries; a metaphysician instructs us in the principles of moral science — principles drawn from facts already known to us. The two processes may take place at the same time — a child in learning a lesson receives both information and instruction — he is taught things he never knew before, and also taught to apply and make use of what he does know already. In fact, pure mathematics is the only branch of instruction which includes no information, as the propositions are all based on principles, previously assumed.

In short, a person who is informed *knows* something he did not know before — one who is instructed *understands* something he did not before — one who is taught can *do* something he could not do before.

Education is more comprehensive than any of the other words before us. It includes the *whole course* of moral and intellectual teaching. One who gives occasional lessons is not said to *educate*. To *educate*, (agreeably to its derivation, from 'e-duco,' not 'in-duco,') includes the *drawing out* of the faculties, so as to teach the pupil how to teach him*self;* which is one of the most valuable of arts.

Moral training, considered *by itself*, is called 'teaching;'

---

* We have here used the nouns instead of the verbs for convenience' sake, as they precisely correspond.

this constitutes no exception to the rule laid down, as its object is to enable us — not to *know* — but to *do* what is right. We see an example of this in Kenn's well-known evening hymn, —

Teach me to *live,* that I may dread, &c.

TO ALLEVIATE, MITIGATE, RELIEVE.

The first two words express a more limited action than the third; or rather, to speak more correctly, the verb 'to relieve' includes both a limited and a complete action; while 'to mitigate' and 'to alleviate' have *only* a limited one. Pain or grief is said to be *relieved* when it is either lessened or entirely removed; when it is alleviated or mitigated, it is *only partially* removed. We might say, 'I hope this remedy will *mitigate* your sufferings, even if it cannot entirely *relieve* them.' 'To relieve' may also be applied either to persons or things. We speak not only of 'relieving a sufferer,' but of 'relieving pain or distress.'

'To mitigate' and 'to alleviate' resemble each other very nearly; but there is a slight shade of difference. 'To alleviate' is only used to describe what is done to others; 'to mitigate' is rather oftener applied to ourselves. We may pursue some course of action to mitigate our *own* sorrow and anxiety; we endeavor to alleviate the sorrow of another.

'Alleviate' is only applied to suffering or distress; 'mitigate' may be used in speaking of the severity of the laws.

TO ANNOUNCE, PROCLAIM, DECLARE.

The arrival of a distinguished person is *announced* — the tidings of a victory are *proclaimed* — a man on trial *declares* his innocence. 'To announce' is applied to persons and tidings, but not to opinions; 'to declare' and 'proclaim,' to tidings and opinions, but not to persons. 'To announce,' extends not only to the present, but to things a little future, or just at hand; an approaching marriage, for example, is announced, but 'to proclaim' and 'to declare' only apply to the present and what is just past. A determination may be either announced, proclaimed, or declared; but when announced, it is merely noticed as about to take place; when proclaimed, published to the world at large, and as it were officially, (a thing can only be proclaimed to a number)—when declared, merely stated openly.

Formerly, 'to declare' meant, to make clear, or to prove: as we may see in the 22d Article of our Church, 'unless it may be *declared* that they be taken from Scripture.'

TO RENOUNCE, RECANT, ABJURE.

'To renounce' is simply to give up or throw aside a possession, a pursuit, or an opinion; we may even renounce a thing we never had, or a pursuit we never followed, if we are capable of having it, are supposed to have had it, or are liable to have or to follow it; as when a child has the promise made for him at his baptism, of 'renouncing the world,' &c. 'To recant' is limited to opinions, and implies *change;* and not only this, but an *open declaration* of having changed the opinion in question, and almost a confession of error. 'To abjure' is applied both to opinions and to allegiance or adherance to any person or party; and it does not necessarily imply any change, as is shown by the formula of *abjuring* all allegiance to the Pope, &c.

Perhaps it may be added, that to abjure, properly speaking, is an act professing to be performed readily and of free will, while a recantation or renunciation may be forced. We might say, 'these two men have changed in a very different way; the one has altered his sentiments and *abjures* his opinions; the other, rather than *renounce* certain privileges, was induced to *recant*.'

'To abjure' also preserves much of its original meaning, (*ab-juro*, to swear against); it always implies a solemn and strong protest against the thing abjured. We may renounce what we think good-for-nothing, or even what we still value; we may recant opinions we in our hearts approve of; we abjure what we detest, or are supposed to detest.

TO UNDERSTAND, TO COMPREHEND.

The former of these verbs is used in a much more extended sense than the latter. Whatever we comprehend, we understand; but 'to understand' is used on many occasions in which to comprehend would be inadmissible. We never speak of 'not *comprehending* a foreign language,' or indistinct speech; in these cases 'understand' would be the correct word. But we may *comprehend* the sense of some deep and abstruse discourse or problem, though 'understand' might also be employed in this sense. It would be quite correct to say, 'I did not *comprehend* his exposition, or his arguments, although I *understood* the language, and the grammatical import of each sentence.'

Some deep and rather hidden meaning seems to be implied by the word 'comprehend;' it preserves something of its old etymology, 'to take in'—and in this sense many English readers are accustomed to take for granted that the word 'incomprehensible' in the Athanasian Creed, implies a deep mystery which cannot be *comprehended:* whereas the word used is an obsolete and *now* incorrect translation of the Latin '*Immensus*,' and should be rendered 'Infinite.'

TO PRAISE, TO ADMIRE, TO COMMEND, TO EXTOL, TO EULOGIZE.

We praise or commend a person for what he *does;* we admire him for what he *is;* we praise his actions; we admire his natural qualities. No natural endowment can be correctly praised or commended. Secondly, 'to admire' relates to feeling rather than to the expression of that feeling; while 'to praise' or 'commend' is the outward expression of sentiments of esteem or approbation. We are said 'to praise' a person in verse; we could not be said to *admire* him in verse, but only to give utterance to our admiration.

'To praise' has also a second and religious meaning, which is the chief distinction between it and the verb 'to commend.' In 'praising God,' it would be impious to conceive that any idea of approbation or commendation could be intended; the expression is nearly synonymous with 'glorify' or 'magnify.'

'To extol,' is to express either praise or admiration in a vehement and high-flown manner: 'to eulogize,' is to do the same thing in a set discourse. The substantive 'eulogy' may be considered as a conjugate to both these verbs.

TO PROMOTE, TO FORWARD.

These words are often, but not uniformly, synonymous.

1st. 'To forward' applies to the *means;* 'to promote,' to the end. A philanthropist is said to *promote*, not forward, the welfare of mankind: he endeavors to *forward* those objects which are undertaken with this view.

2dly. 'To promote' is often used in relation to some effect which is only *beginning* to be produced, while 'to forward' would be used when the cause was actually in operation. For instance: 'I have taken great pains to *promote* education in an uncivilized and ignorant district, and the contributions of my friends have done much to *forward* my views.'

TO BE, TO EXIST.

These two verbs are often used in a nearly similar sense:

but 'to exist' refers more to the original nature of things than 'to be.' If we say, 'there could not *be* freedom of the press under a despotic government,' we merely imply that it would not be *allowed;* but the phrase 'freedom of the press could not *exist* under a despotic government,' would imply an inherent incompatibility in the *nature* of the two institutions.

TO REMARK, TO OBSERVE.

These verbs are used sometimes to describe the act of the mind, and sometimes the *expression* of that act: in this last sense they are nearly if not quite synonymous.

But where the mental act is the thing referred to, the verb 'to observe' is more general, 'to remark' more particular. We should say, in reference to any natural phenomenon, 'I *observe* that such and such a law generally prevails; I *remarked* several instances of it.' 'I *observe* he has a harsh and cold demeanor; if you watch you will *remark* proofs of it.' In this last clause, 'to observe' might have been used instead of 'to remark:' but we do not usually speak of 'remarking' a general principle.

We speak of 'a habit of observing;' of 'the advantage of knowing how to observe,' &c.; in neither of these cases could the verb 'to remark' be substituted.

TO ENDUE, TO ENDOW.

'To endue,' is limited to mental qualifications: 'to endow' also includes physical and worldly ones: indeed, primarily it refers to property, and is only figuratively extended to qualities of the mind or person. An institution is richly endowed; a person is endowed with beauty, strength, talents, &c.: he is endued only with *mental* qualifications.

TO SHUN, AVOID, ELUDE.

We shun a person we dislike or dread: we avoid either

a person, a thing, an action or course of action; we elude search or pursuit only. 'To elude' always implies literally or figuratively an attempt to defeat efforts to seek or follow us; and it also implies (as its root *e-ludo* does) a round-about and indirect way of escape. The prisoner we read of, who was set by the Indians to run for his life, would not be said to elude pursuit as long as his course was on an open plain; as soon as he had recourse to the bushes and sought concealment, the word might be applicable.

To shun or avoid, on the other hand, are hardly ever used when a search is implied. To shun is always personal; for when we speak of 'shunning vice,' &c. a personification is always implied. It also indicates a more pointed and marked endeavor to keep out of a person's way than 'to avoid.' 'To avoid' is used in a more abstract sense than either 'shun' or 'elude;' we not only avoid persons and things, but trouble, thought, &c.

Lastly, 'to avoid'* and 'to elude' both generally, if not always, imply *success:* which 'shun' does not. 'To shun' is only to *seek* to avoid. We might say, 'I have constantly *shunned* him, but I cannot *avoid* meeting him sometimes, for I cannot *elude* his continued pursuit of me.'

TO AMAZE, TO ASTONISH.

'To astonish' merely implies, to affect very strongly with overpowering wonder. 'To amaze' generally conveys the impression of some degree of perplexity or bewilderment. It may be said, to use a colloquialism, that we 'do not know what to make' of anything that amazes us. We are *astonished* at some marvel of nature or art: we are *amazed* when a person's conduct is quite different from what we expected.

The immediate root of this last verb — the word 'maze'

---

* Originally, to *make void,* or of no effect.

— conveys the idea of entanglement and bewilderment, whether mental or material.

In the West of England, 'mazed' is the expression used among the common people for 'mad,' still implying the same notion of entanglement in the brain.

TO EMPLOY, TO MAKE USE OF.

'To employ' generally, though not always, implies some degree of co-operation, or at least of *consciousness* in the agent. 'To make use of' implies a *passive* agency. We employ an amanuensis — we make use of a pen. Hence, when a person is said to 'make use' of another, it generally implies an idea degrading or insulting towards the agent; which would not be conveyed by the word 'employ.' A person is *made use* of unconsciously, or perhaps even against his will. A confidential second is employed by his superior: a tool in the hands of an intriguer is *made use* of. Hence, we speak of a person's employing *himself*, but *making use* of his *faculties*.

Both these words, correctly speaking, imply the use of means to an end, and do not apply to any act which is *itself* the end. Hence the expression common among the lower classes of Irish, 'to *make use* of food,' sounds anomalous in the ears of strangers. It is true that the act of taking food, and of inhaling air, is a means used for the purpose of supporting life; but in breathing and eating this is not contemplated at the moment, these acts being instinctive: therefore, the expression 'to make use of' does not apply to them.

SHALL, WILL.

These two verbs have undergone curious alterations. In very old English, 'shall' indicated simple futurity, and 'will' intention.

At the time our Bible translation was made, the language in this respect was in a state of transition; in some cases, the two verbs were used in the old sense, while in others they were applied nearly in our modern acceptation. For instance: in 2 Kings, we read — 'Ahab *shall* slay me,' and in Gal. v. 'Walk in the spirit and ye *shall* not fulfil the lusts of the flesh.'

In both these sentences, 'will' would be used in modern English; and in many others a misapprehension of the real meaning of the sacred writers is induced by a forgetfulness of this difference. But then, again, in John xvi. 2, we have 'Whosoever killeth you *will* think that he doeth God service:' 'will' is here employed exactly as it would be in modern English.

It is difficult to define intelligibly to a foreigner the modern use of these two words, though throughout the whole of *England* no misuse of them can be observed, even among the lowest of the people.* But in Ireland they are constantly reversed, and in Scotland 'will' is used improperly, though 'shall' is not.

In our modern use of these verbs, we have curiously divided the persons of each. '*I will*, *you shall*, *he shall*,' denotes a futurity connected with *the will of the speaker*: while, '*I shall*, *you will*, *he will*,' implies a futurity unconnected with the speaker's resolve. For instance, we should say, 'I will go, you shall go, he shall go' — but 'I shall die, you will die, he will die.'

We always say, 'I *shall* attain such an age next birthday:' if 'will' were substituted, it would imply a power of volun-

* The expression common in the West of England, 'I *will* if *I shall*,' cannot be considered an exception; for it is an ellipse for 'I will if *you say that* I shall.'

tarily determining our age. 'You *shall* have some money to-morrow' implies 'I will procure it for you.' 'You *will* have it,' indicates an expectation quite independent of the speaker's intentions. When, however, *will* is emphatic, so that one would write it underscored, or in italics, as denoting *resolute determination*, it has the same sense in all three persons; as, for instance,—'I [or you, or he] *will* take this course, whatever may be said to the contrary.' The opposite to 'will' in this sense, is not 'shall' but 'must;' as, 'I [or you, or he] must submit to this, however unwillingly.'

There are some cases in which either 'shall' or 'will' might be used, but in which the meaning would be modified according to the word employed. In answering a request, '*I will*,' indicates compliance; '*I shall*' would convey an intention of doing the thing asked, quite independently of any wish to gratify the asker. 'I *shall* go,' indicates simple futurity—'I *will* go,' both futurity and a determined intention. 'I shall go,' in a case where we *are* determined, expresses therefore *less* than we mean: and we sometimes use this form of *under-stating* our meaning,—or what the Greeks called *Eironeia*,—to express very strong resolution. Hence the common expression—'I shall do no such thing'—'He won't make me do so'—which are often used to convey the strongest idea of determination, and therefore, at first sight, appear exceptions to the rules here laid down.

TO REND, TO TEAR.

'To rend' differs from 'to tear;' first, in implying *voluntary* action, never accidental, while 'tear' may apply to either. We may *tear* a dress in falling down: an eastern mourner *rends* his garments to express grief. We do, indeed, speak of rocks being rent by an earthquake or sails by the wind,* but the natural agent is always supposed to be personified.

Secondly, 'to rend' always implies splitting or dividing: we are said to tear, not rend the hair: an exile is torn, not rent, from his native land. A tree is *rent* by lightning, and *torn* up by the roots by a high wind.

---

* See the lines in Scott's *Marmion*, canto vi.:—

> 'The pennon sunk and rose;
> As bends the bark's mast in the gale,
> When *rent* are rigging, shrouds, and sail,
> It wavered 'mid the foes.'

ADJECTIVES.

CIVIL, POLITE, COURTEOUS, POLISHED, WELL-BRED.

Civility is *now* something less than politeness or courtesy. In old English it was used for elegance, or polish in general (see *Pilgrim's Progress*). It now implies that attention to others which is *absolutely* necessary, and no more. If a servant-maid, or a workman, is spoken of as being *civil*, it is considered as a term of approbation, because no more is expected from them ; but with the higher classes *civility* ought to be taken for granted, and something more of *prévenance* and polish of manners is expected.

The difference between ' courtesy ' on the one hand, and ' politeness ' and ' polish ' on the other, — is, that courtesy has more reference to others — politeness to ourselves. We may say indifferently, ' He received me ' *courteously*,' or ' He received me *politely*,' — but in the one case we should be dwelling on the attention he was paying to *us*, as a part of his duty to us, — and in the other, on the behavior assumed by him from proper self-respect. Courtesy, then, seems to imply more kindliness of feeling. Politeness has, indeed, been defined as ' benevolence in trifles,' — but this outward benevolence may spring merely from outward regard for the opinion of the world, without real kindness of heart. Hence, St. Peter does not recommend us ' to be ' polite,' but to be ' courteous,' because he is treating of our duty towards our neighbours, not of what is due to ourselves. In short, a man is polite for *himself* — courteous for *others*.

Polish refers even more completely to ourselves than *politeness.* We should not speak of 'behaving to such a person in a *polished* manner,' but 'politely.' In short, 'politeness' occupies a place half-way between 'polish' and 'courtesy.' 'Polish' also implies a high degree of elegance and refinement, and cannot exist without considerable cultivation; it seems, as it were, to belong to artificial life.

'Well-bred' is rather referable to general conduct than to particular actions. A *well-bred* person will behave *politely* to others. It also implies general propriety of behavior, whether connected with others or not. 'Ill-bred,' on the other hand, is oftener applied to individual actions than 'well-bred,' though it applies equally to general conduct. We say, 'that is a very *ill-bred* speech,' but we should not speak of a *well-bred* speech, but rather of well-bred conduct and deportment. It originally referred to a good early education, and still indicates that conduct and those manners which would be the *natural effect* of such an education.

GRACEFUL, ELEGANT.

Grace is in a great measure a natural gift; *elegance* implies cultivation, or something of a more artificial character. A rustic, uneducated girl may be graceful; but an elegant woman must be accomplished and well trained. It is the same with things as with persons; we talk of a graceful tree, but of an *elegant* house or other building. Animals may be graceful, but they cannot be elegant. The movements of a kitten, or a young fawn, are full of grace; but to call them *elegant* animals would be absurd. Lastly, 'elegant' may be applied to mental qualifications, which 'graceful' never can. Elegance must always imply something that is *made* or invented by man. An *imitation of nature* is not called so; therefore we do not speak of an 'elegant picture,' though we do of an elegant pattern for a gown, an elegant piece of work.

With respect to the other fine arts, it is a curious fact, that though music and poetry are both reckoned as the offspring of the mind, yet the term 'elegant,' which is constantly applied to a poem, is not admitted in speaking of a piece of music. The reason of this may perhaps be, that poetry is really more emphatically the production of the mind than music. If disagreeable images, or discordant metres, are introduced, the poetry is bad, but still it *is* poetry, and the fault that we find with it rests on the very fact of its being such. On the other hand, music is called bad if it is feeble, heavy, or tasteless; but unless the musical notes are selected in obedience to certain laws, they are *not* music. Strictly speaking, false chords should not be denominated 'bad music,' but no music at all. The laws of melody and harmony are laws of nature, as immutable as the laws of gravitation. The musician has a large choice of various combinations, but not an unlimited one; he must adhere to these laws, and is not permitted to invent any combination of notes at variance with them.

But whether this difference between music and poetry be considered as altogether holding good or not, certain it is that music seems to be regarded as belonging more to nature than to art. Melodies are discovered, rather than invented; and hence, while 'graceful' is a term often used in reference to them, 'elegant' is not.

When used in connection with the productions of the intellect, 'elegant' is always applied to the lighter branches of study. 'An elegant scholar,' 'elegant literature,' are terms always implying a reference to the *Belles Lettres.* Lastly, 'elegant' is applied to a kind of merit which consists rather in the absence of glaring faults than in striking beauties. An elegant poem is smooth and well-constructed, but not a work of original genius. 'Graceful,' on the other hand, is frequently applied to *bodily* movements; which scarcely ever is the case with elegant. Even in speaking of movements which are acquired, and therefore to a certain extent artificial, the word 'graceful' is used instead of 'elegant;' as a graceful dancer; a graceful manner of doing the honors of a table. This sense of the word forms, perhaps, an exception to the general rule — that elegance is the characteristic of art, and grace of nature.

'Grace' originally meant 'favor,' and the derivative, 'gracious,' has preserved the same meaning. The religious sense of the word was evidently from the same origin.

BEAUTIFUL, HANDSOME, PRETTY, LOVELY, FINE.

'Beautiful' includes all the other terms of admiration mentioned here: and is stronger than any of them, except, perhaps, 'lovely.' From being generally opposed to the *sublime*, it has gradually come to imply a certain degree of softness and delicacy which makes it inapplicable to a man, for whom the only terms of admiration are 'handsome' and 'fine.'

'Handsome' implies — 1st. Not exactly an artificial beauty, but the beauty of some person or thing which is *trained* or *cultivated*. We speak of a 'handsome' man or woman, a 'handsome' house, a 'handsome' horse, or dog, or tree; but we should not speak of a 'handsome' wild animal, or a 'handsome' prospect: (though these expressions are incorrectly used by the Irish and Americans.)

2dly. 'Handsome' implies beauty on a large scale. A lady who is very *petite* and slight in figure, an infant, or a small animal, is never called 'handsome.'

3dly. It excludes the highest degree of beauty; and the same is the case when applied to moral conduct. 'Handsome behavior' is behavior that is liberal, fair, right, honorable: but a heroically generous action would never be called 'handsome.'

'Pretty' is applied to external beauty on a small scale, and never of a very high order. It implies softness and delicacy, and is therefore never used for a man except in contempt.

'Lovely' implies something more than mere external beauty. It may be applied to the mind as well as the person. We usually understand by it personal beauty and pleasing manners combined. A woman who is disagreeable and ungraceful would never be called a 'lovely' woman, however faultless her features may be.

'Fine' is perhaps a more puzzling word than any of the group. Its original sense was that of something delicate, subtle, slender, *fin*, in short; and this has been preserved in one sense of the word, in speaking, for example, of a 'fine' edge, a 'fine' sense of touch or hearing, a 'fine' thread, &c. But its other and commonest meaning is,—beauty of rather a large and coarse kind—the *reverse* of delicate. A 'fine' face is one with a bold and strongly marked contour; a 'fine' child is a stout, rosy, healthy child; a 'fine' woman is one whose features and figure are rather on a large scale.

'Fine' in its third sense implies over-fastidious, proud, ready to give oneself airs. The conjugate word, *finery*, is nearest to this sense of the word. Its origin was probably the Latin *finis*, an end; it was first transferred to an *edge* or sharp point, and thence to something subtle and delicate.

'Fine' in the sense of an *amende*, a sum of money paid down as a penalty, has probably the same root; the end of a trial or lawsuit being the payment of the forfeited sum.

SINCERE, HONEST, UPRIGHT.

'Sincerity' *may* be used in two senses; and this leads to much ambiguity in reasoning. It may either mean, on the one hand, reality of conviction and earnestness of purpose, — or, on the other, purity from all unfairness or dishonesty. Many people overlook this; they will speak of a man's being 'sincere,' when they mean he has a real conviction that his end is a good one, — and imagine this must imply that he is 'honest;' whereas, he may be 'sincere' in his desire to gain his end, and *dishonest* in the means he employs for that end. 'Honest,' on the other hand, is not an ambiguous term; it implies straightforwardness and fairness of conduct. 'Upright,' implies honesty and dignity of character; it is the opposite of 'meanness,' as 'honesty' is of 'shuffling' or 'insincerity.'*

WONDERFUL, STRANGE, SURPRISING, ADMIRABLE, CURIOUS.

We *admire* what is excellent, noble, glorious, eminent; we are, properly speaking, *surprised* simply at what is *unexpected;* we *wonder* at what is extraordinary, lofty, great, or striking, although it may not be unexpected.

An intelligent mind will be filled with wonder while contemplating many of the works of nature, although they may be well known, and even familiar.

The word 'strange' refers, as well as 'wonderful,' to something in itself uncommon; but 'wonderful' is applied to something great or noble, something, in short, *above* the common; while 'strange' signifies rather what is *beside* the common — in short, something *odd.* We should not say, in speaking of the higher and more sublime phenomena of the creation, that they are 'strange,' but that they are 'wonderful;' but any oddity or freak of nature, on a smaller scale, we call 'strange.'

Nothing that awakens any feeling of awe or sublimity, or any poetical feeling, would be called 'strange;' hence it

* 'Upright' may be considered as the conjugate of the substantive 'rectitude.'

often happens that new and remarkable natural phenomena, or striking discoveries, awaken a sentiment of *wonder* in thoughtful and inquiring minds, while the vulgar and thoughtless designate them as 'very strange.'

Lastly, what is positively unpleasant to the eye or mind may be 'strange,' but not 'wonderful.' We speak of '*wonderfully* beautiful,' but of '*strangely* ugly.'

'Curious' means something 'wonderful' on a *small scale;* it is perhaps nearer to 'strange' in its meaning, but does not exclude the idea of beauty. The minute parts of a leaf or flower are at once 'curious' and beautiful. In old English, 'strange' was used where 'wonderful' would now be employed. Shakspeare speaks of '*strange* swiftness.'

SILLY, FOOLISH, ABSURD, WEAK, STUPID, SIMPLE, DULL.

'Silly' is most commonly applied to words, writings, manners, or character; 'foolish' to actions. We speak of a 'silly' book, a 'silly' speech, a 'silly' manner; but seldom of taking a 'silly' step, committing a 'silly' action; in these last cases, we use the word 'foolish.' 'Silly' very frequently, though not always, implies *deficiency* of intellect or feebleness of character; 'foolish' an *abuse* of intellect. A 'foolish' man is one who does not make use of the sense he possesses. More of blame is implied in the word 'foolish;' more of contempt in 'silly.'

'Weak' implies some moral deficiency; a weak man is one who either wants sufficient firmness to maintain his principles, or wants clearness of *moral sense* to perceive distinctly what is right.

'Absurd,' applied to an action, implies something laughable. An absurd person is one who commits ridiculous acts of folly.

'Stupid' is used merely to express a lumpish, heavy,

cloudy perception of everything proceeding from a want of intellect. It is entirely a negative quality.

'Dull' is not quite the same; it implies slowness, but not necessarily deficiency of intellect. A boy who is slow and dull in learning may, nevertheless, be not wanting in sense, and may be able to understand a subject well, when once he has mastered its difficulties.

'Simple,' when it is applied to an act of folly, implies a want of quicksightedness — of what the French call *savoir faire*, springing either from natural deficiency or want of experience. The French *bonhommie* and the Greek *Euthes* are used to signify the same thing.

JOYFUL, GLAD, PLEASED, DELIGHTED, GRATIFIED.

'Joyful,' and its conjugate word, 'joy,' are used for the highest degree of pleasure, and always for pleasure excited by some external event. They are in their nature transient; though 'joys' is used in a different sense, implying a very high degree of pleasure, whether externally excited at the moment or not.

'Glad' is the lowest degree of pleasure; it answers to 'sorry,' as an opposite term — like 'sorry,' too, it was used in a stronger sense in old English: 'Then are they *glad*, because they are at rest.' (Psalm cvii.)

'Pleased' may imply either gladness or approbation. 'Delighted' is a much stronger expression of the same feeling.

'Gratified' always refers to a pleasure conferred by some human agent, but is not the same as 'grateful.' 'Grateful' refers to the feeling of the recipient towards the donor; 'gratified' implies a sense of pleasure modified by the consideration that in part we owe it to another.

Conjugate words. — 'Joyous' is used for a mood of the mind — a state of feeling occasioned by high animal spirits.

'Enjoy' is used in a lower sense; it merely implies a sense of the pleasures around us. 'Enjoyment,' when used alone, is rather lower still — more connected with the pleasures of the senses. A cow grazing in a rich pasture would be said to be in a state of 'enjoyment.'

'To rejoice' is nearly the same as 'to be glad,' but stronger. 'To gladden' is decidedly stronger than 'glad:' it preserves more of the early meaning of the word; and so does 'gladness.'

'Gratification' is not exactly the same as 'gratified;' it does not necessarily imply that the pleasure is conferred by another person. It is frequently used for sensual enjoyment — as, 'the *gratifications* of the palate.' 'To gratify' is sometimes used for satisfying a desire — as, 'to *gratify* the appetite;' still more for a mental passion — as, 'to *gratify* vanity or ambition.'

IDLE, LAZY, INDOLENT, SLOTHFUL.

'Slothful' and 'indolent' are applied to a general slowness and languor, and hatred of movement or exertion. An 'indolent' person likes always to remain quiet. A 'lazy' person is one who is *disposed* to be *idle.* It is more applied to the disposition itself; 'idleness' to a tendency to yield to it. But an 'idle' person may be active in his way; he may even be very persevering in following up some scheme of his own; but he will be reluctant to force himself to do what he does not like, and he will seldom like *continuous* exertion of any kind. Many idle boys will work very hard at their own sports, and take great pains to leap, run, or play at games; but neglect their lessons. A lazy person, on the other hand, may employ himself, but will dislike the trouble of getting up to fetch a dictionary if he is learning a lesson, or of going to consult some person who might help him in the business he is transacting; and to spare himself the exertion, he will be obliged to work harder in the end: hence the proverb, that '*lazy* people take the most trouble.'

'Lazy' may be considered as the opposite to 'alert.'

'Slothful' and 'indolent' as opposed to 'active.'

'Idle' as opposed to 'busy,' and 'negligent' to 'diligent.'

GRATEFUL, THANKFUL.

'Grateful' is an expression most commonly used in reference to a *human agent* who has conferred some special favor on us. 'Thankful' is more commonly applied to express our feeling of the goodness of Providence. One who makes an ill return for the kindness of a benefactor is 'ungrateful;' one who is forgetful of the mercies shown him by his Creator is 'unthankful.' 'Thankfulness' and 'unthankfulness' are more used to describe the state of a person's mind: 'gratitude,' and still more, 'ingratitude,' for the *conduct springing* from the state of mind. This, perhaps, follows from the first proposition, as we cannot make any *return* for the benefits of Providence, and can only prove our gratitude by the state of our minds. 'Grateful' however, is more applied to disposition, and less to conduct, than 'ungrateful.'

FRUITLESS, USELESS, INEFFECTUAL, VAIN.

'Fruitless' is generally applied to an undertaking which fails, not from its being ill-calculated to produce good effects, but from some unexpected hinderance or calamity arising to frustrate it. For example, 'Such an one has made a *fruitless* attempt to dissuade his friend from the rash step he was about to take;' here the attempt is supposed to fail, not from its being unwise or ill-judged, but from the obstinacy or folly of the person advised.

'Useless,' on the other hand, is applied to undertakings which are in themselves ill-calculated for success.

We should say to a very self-willed person, 'It is *useless* to advise you'—meaning, 'your character makes such attempts utterly hopeless, and it is ill-advised of any one who knows you to make them.'

A bad crab-tree, and an apple-tree spoilt by a blight, are equally unlikely to produce good fruit; but the first it is 'useless,' the second 'fruitless,' to attempt to improve.

'Ineffectual' nearly resembles 'fruitless,' but implies a failure of a less hopeless character. We might say, 'I desisted, finding all my efforts *fruitless:*' but 'after several *ineffectual* efforts I at last succeeded.'

'Vain,' in the sense in which we are now considering it, is nearly synonymous with 'fruitless.'

FRANK, OPEN, CANDID, INGENUOUS.

'Open' is generally applied to dispositions, not to speeches. An 'open' disposition merely implies a disposition to speak out what is in the mind—a difficulty in concealment.

'Frank,' on the other hand, is oftener applied to words or manners, though a disposition is sometimes called 'frank.' It is a more *active* quality, so to speak, than 'openness.' A timid person may be open; one who is 'frank' must be bold and fearless: it is sometimes used for a freedom of speech that borders on bluntness.

'Ingenuous' implies a moral quality; it includes both openness and candor. A person who is open merely from deficiency in natural reserve, would not be necessarily called 'ingenuous;' and '*dis*ingenuous' is always used as a term of blame.

'Candor' signifies fairness of mind—readiness to acknowledge an error. One who can see what is right, and cast aside all prejudice in owning it, is 'candid.' It implies, indeed, nearly the same disposition as 'ingenuous.'*

RASH, FOOL-HARDY.

'Rashness' is, correctly speaking, applied to some risk encountered for the sake of something in itself important, though not so as to be adequate to the danger incurred. To be 'fool-hardy,' on the other hand, is to run a risk for the sake of some trifling and unimportant object, or from mere wantonness. For instance, a soldier who should charge an overwhelming body of the enemy at the head of a handful of men, would be 'rash:' but one who should expose himself to a battery of cannon, merely to obtain a draught of water, would be 'fool-hardy.'

TRANSIENT, TRANSITORY, FLEETING.

What is 'transient' is in itself momentary and short in duration; what is 'transitory' is *liable* to pass away. The one expression directs attention to its shortness, the other to its uncertainty. All earthly pleasures are 'transitory;' the diversions which yield but momentary amusements are 'transient,' or 'fleeting.' These two words are nearly alike: but 'fleeting' refers rather to the fact of their being *in the act* of passing away, 'transient' to their shortness of stay. 'Transient' and 'fleeting' may also be applied to objects of sight, as light or colors: 'transitory' only to abstract things.

---

* The Greeks do not appear to have had any word answering to 'candid.' In the Greek Testament the word *gennaios*, noble, or generous, is used in describing the fairness of mind with which the Bereans searched the Scriptures

5

BRIGHT, SHINING, SPARKLING, BRILLIANT, GLISTENING, GLITTERING.

Of these words, two, 'sparkling' and brilliant,' especially the latter, are very frequently used in a figurative sense. We speak of 'brilliant talents' as often as of a 'brilliant gem.' The two first words, on the other hand, 'bright' and 'shining,' are *usually* applied only to the literal effects of light; though they, too, are occasionally used figuratively. 'Bright' has the most extended signification of all these words, and includes them all. 'Shining' is most commonly applied to the effect of light on a smooth or polished surface.

'Sparkling' is used for the fitful and rapid emission of *points* or flashes of light. It is figuratively applied to those mental powers which show themselves in rapid, sudden scintillations: as 'sparkling wit,' or gaiety. A diamond, or finely cut piece of crystal, is 'sparkling;' the sea often sparkles in the sun; a plate of polished metal is 'shining;' but both would be called 'bright.'

'Brilliant' is a stronger expression than 'bright,' when used in its literal sense. 'Bright' and 'shining' are now scarce ever used figuratively, (unless the modern expression, 'a bright face,' 'a bright smile,' be considered as such,) except in a negative sense, as 'he is not very *bright*,' 'he has no *shining talents*.'

'Glittering' implies a fitful, scintillating light, but less *concentrated* and intense, and more broken and scattered than what we describe as 'sparkling.' An *icicle* is 'glittering;' a *diamond* is 'sparkling.' The human eye is not usually said to 'glitter,' but to 'sparkle,' except when a wild, unsteady glance is indicated.

'Glistening,' on the other hand, implies a soft and yet

fitful light, modified by moisture. The moonbeams 'glisten' on the water, the eyes through tears.

TIMID, COWARDLY, TIMOROUS, DASTARDLY.

'Timid' is applied both to the state of mind (sometimes transient) in which a person may happen to be at the moment, and to the habitual disposition; 'timorous,' only to the disposition. 'Timid' is, therefore, the more extensive term, and comprehends the meanings of 'timorous' as well as its own. Both are equally applied to a dread of *personal* danger; but 'timorous' is oftener used for *moral* danger than 'timid.' Both are equally applied to character. 'Cowardly' and 'dastardly' are used alike for character and conduct, and both as terms of strong reproach. 'Dastardly' implies meanness as well as cowardice. 'Cowardice' is merely timidity carried into action. A timid man may be led by strong motives to perform individual acts of bravery; a timid mother will often incur great risks for her children; but a *cowardly* person can never on any occasion act bravely; 'cowardice,' therefore implies a character more completely governed by fear than mere 'timidity.' 'Timid,' in short, may be said to denote the *disposition*, and 'cowardly' the *habit*.

MILD, GENTLE, MEEK, SOFT.

Of these four words, 'meek' is the only one which is *exclusively* employed in a *moral* sense; the other three may be either moral or physical in their signification.

'Soft' denotes an influence which is *weak but pleasant*. A soft voice, a soft light, are in themselves agreeable. But it is not consistent with the highest degree of power, or indeed, with *great force* of any kind. A powerful voice, however sweet-toned, would not be commonly denominated 'soft.' A soft color cannot be bright or intense. The term '*soft* music' is applied generally to music which pleases without exciting or enrapturing. Milton has preserved this meaning in his *Allegro* —

'Lap me in *soft* Lydian airs.'

In this line he describes music as an agreeable *accompaniment* to other pleasures; he uses very different language when he describes in the *Penseroso* the higher effects of music.

'Mild' and 'gentle' are more negative in their meaning. In their primary sense, they merely imply an influence which does not act with an unpleasant force. A gentle voice is one that is *not loud;* mild air, air that is *not sharp*, or *cold*. If there is an exception to this rule, it is in the case of disposition or temper, in which 'gentleness' seems to imply a more positively amiable and pleasing quality than 'mildness.' (The substantives and adjectives have here exactly corresponding meanings.)

In manners, 'mildness' and 'gentleness' are consistent with dignity of deportment, which 'softness' is not.

'Meekness' differs from the other three words in being applied to the temper only, never to mere manners and deportment. It is a word which has undergone some change. In former times, (as may be seen from the use made of it in the Bible,) it denoted a religious patience and submission to injuries and humility before God. It is evidently in this sense that Moses is spoken of as the 'meekest of men.' In modern times, it may be said to be used in two different senses, and while the strictly *theological* meaning (if we may so express it) is pretty much what it formerly was, its secondary and ordinary colloquial meaning, in conformity with the tendency to degenerate which may be observed in all words descriptive of virtues, has come to signify a (especially when applied to a man) somewhat *excessive* disposition to yield and submit.

This ambiguity is perhaps to be regretted, as it attaches a ludicrous or contemptible signification to a word, which originally and properly denoted a virtue peculiarly belonging to the people of God. In its oldest and most correct *religious* sense, it always implied humility; in which it was distinguished from the other three words under consideration. A person may be soft and mild in manners, without real humility or sweetness of temper. Many think that a woman whose manners are very soft must necessarily be meek, whereas softness is consistent even with self-will and obstinacy.

DIFFERENT, UNLIKE, DISSIMILAR, DISTINCT.

The word 'different' calls the attention to the separation into classes. Things are called 'different,' from the circumstance that they cannot be mistaken for each other, or confounded together; they are not viewed as necessarily opposed, but as having qualities which keep them apart. We may say, 'These things are *different*, and yet not *unlike*.' The word 'unlike' calls the attention to opposition or contrast in the things compared; and this more particularly when they do *not* belong to separate classes. We should say, 'These two sisters are so *unlike*, that one would suppose they belonged to *different* families.' In short, things are said to be 'unlike,' when they might be *expected* to be 'like;' 'different,' when non-resemblance is in the natural course of things.

'Different,' however, is rendered more puzzling by its having, in fact, *two* meanings, corresponding exactly to the two meanings of the word SAME,* one of which implies *similarity*, the other *identity*. The two senses of the word 'different' are precisely opposed, relatively, to these

* See Appendix to Whately's *Logic*.

meanings of 'same' — one, signifying *non-identity;* the other, *non-similarity.* In the first sense, we might say, 'These are two *different* dresses, made of exactly the same material;' in the other, 'They are of very *different* colors.'

'Dissimilar' is nearly the same as 'unlike,' but less strong, as is generally the case with words of Latin origin, when contrasted with Saxon ones.

'Distinct' is nearly the same as 'different,' but is chiefly used with abstract terms.

ROMANTIC, SENTIMENTAL.

Both these terms are used to express the effects of ill-directed or excessive feeling and imagination; but in romance the imagination, in sentiment the feelings have the predominance. A 'romantic' scheme is one which is wild, impracticable, and yet contains something which captivates the fancy. A romantic mind loves to dwell on adventures and dazzling enterprises, and on such incidents as would grace a wild fiction or a poem, and delights in every action, every event, that can be invested with a picturesque or dramatic character.*

A 'sentimental' mind, on the other hand, is rather prone to over-wrought feeling and exaggerated tenderness. The sickly compassion or benevolence which expands itself in lamentations instead of actions — the weak and foolish manifestations of love or friendship, come under the head of 'sentimentality.'

The 'Romantic' may be considered as the less dangerous of these two tendencies: a certain degree of romance is commonly found in young people when the imagination is active and the temperament enthusiastic; and it is then

---

* See Foster's Essay on this word.

easily subdued by experience and reason. 'Sentimentality' is the characteristic of a weaker mind, and is therefore less curable. It is easier to correct an abuse of imagination than an abuse of feeling.

AUTHENTIC, GENUINE.

Bishop Watson thus distinguishes between things 'authentic' and things 'genuine.'

'A *genuine* book is that which was written by the person whose name it bears, as the author of it. An *authentic* book is that which relates matters of fact as they really happened; a book may be *genuine* without being *authentic*, and a book may be *authentic* without being *genuine*. The books [written by] Richardson and Fielding are *genuine* books, though the histories of *Clarissa* and *Tom Jones* are fables. *The history of the Island of Formosa* is a *genuine* book: it was written by Psalmanazar; but it is not an *authentic* book, (though it was long esteemed as such, and translated into different languages;) for the author, in the latter part of his life, took shame to himself for having imposed upon the world, and confessed that it was a mere romance. *Anson's Voyage* may de considered as an *authentic* book: it probably contains a true narrative of the principal events recorded in it; but it is not a *genuine* book, having not been written by Walter, to whom it is ascribed, but by Robins.'

SECRET, HIDDEN, CONCEALED, COVERT.

What is 'secret' may be accidentally or unintentially so: 'hidden' and 'concealed' imply something *intentionally* kept secret. We speak of 'a *hidden* plot,' a '*concealed* intention.' 'Covert' is something not *avowed*. It may be *intended* to be seen; 'a *covert* allusion' is meant to be understood, but is not openly expressed.

'Secret' is opposed to 'well-known;' 'hidden' and 'concealed' to 'open;' 'covert' to 'avowed' or 'displayed.'

EVERLASTING, ETERNAL.

Both these terms imply endless duration: but 'eternal' extends to something more — that, viz., which has always existed. Many infidel writers hold that the world is 'eternal' — that is, that it never had a beginning. The heathens believed that their gods were 'everlasting' — *i. e.*, immortal. but not 'eternal,' for their birth and origin were always recorded.

'Everlasting' is, in old English, used improperly for 'eternal,' as in the Psalms, 'Thou art from *everlasting*,' &c.

DURABLE, LASTING, PERMANENT.

'Lasting' is generally applied in an abstract sense — as, 'a *lasting* remembrance,' 'a *lasting* effect:' 'durable' oftener to sensible objects — as, 'a *durable* material;' 'permanent,' to both, but with different varieties of meaning. When applied to abstract subjects, and compared with 'lasting,' it implies something which is established and intended to remain — not intended to be removed or changed; as, 'a *permanent* situation,' 'a *permanent* resting-place.' When applied to tangible objects, on the other hand, and contrasted with 'durable,' 'permanent' means something that remains as it is, and will not wear out *of itself*. 'A permanent dye' or color in painting is one which will not fade or be changed by time. 'Durable,' on the other hand, is oftener applied to *texture*, and always to something which will *endure*, not time alone, but wear and tear; a 'durable' stuff will bear rough handling, and can be worn long.

CONTINUAL, CONTINUOUS, PERPETUAL.

A 'continuous' action is one which is uninterrupted, and goes on unceasingly *as long as it lasts*, though that time may be longer or shorter. 'Continual' is that which is constantly renewed and recurring, though it may be interrupted as frequently as it is renewed. A storm of wind or rain, which never intermits an instant, is 'continuous;' a succession of showers is 'continual.' 'If I am exposed to *continual* interruptions, I cannot pursue a *continuous* train of thought.'

'Perpetual' is sometimes used in the sense of 'continual,' but has rather a stronger signification, implying something which is still *more* constantly recurring. It also means something which is at once continuous and lasting; as, 'the perpetual motion.'

TALKATIVE, LOQUACIOUS, GARRULOUS.

A little child just learning to speak may be 'talkative;' a lively woman may be 'loquacious;' an old man in his dotage is often garrulous.' 'Talkative' implies a continual desire to speak, which may exist without ever saying much at a time; 'loquacious' includes this, and also implies a great flow of words at command. A 'garrulous' person indulges in prosy, tiresome, and lengthy talk, with frequent repetition and needless minuteness of detail. Justice Shallow is represented as 'talkative,' having little or nothing to say, but constantly speaking. Miss Mitford, in her picture of 'the talking lady,' gives an exact picture of a 'loquacious' person. Homer represents old Nestor as 'garrulous.' 'Talkativeness' and 'loquacity' often proceed from high animal spirits, and often, also, from that combination described by phrenologists as an active temperament with an inferior mental development. 'Garrulity' generally arises from feebleness of mind and uncontrolled egotism.

STRONG, POWERFUL, VIGOROUS, FORCIBLE, POTENT.

Of these five terms, the first two alone are applied to

physical force. But they are applied to it in somewhat different senses; 'strong' being the more comprehensive of the two. A 'powerful' man must be 'strong,' but a 'strong person is not necessarily 'powerful.' 'Strong' is more appropriately used to describe a person of sound, firm constitution, capable of enduring fatigue; 'powerful,' one who is able to exert his physical force actively, and to perform feats of strength. 'Power' is almost always active in its signification. 'Strength' is both active and passive. (The two substantives exactly correspond to their adjectives, 'strong' and 'powerful.') The same analogy is preserved when these words are applied to mental qualifications. A 'strong' mind is firm, capable of sustaining shocks, — not easily shaken; a 'powerful' mind is something more — capable of great active efforts, as well as passive endurance, and fitted to command and influence others.

'Vigorous,' in accordance with its root '*vigere*,' implies powers (either of mind or body) in an *active* state: hence we speak of a *vigorous* (not powerful) shoot of a tree. Thus, too, it is applied to *temporary* conditions; we might say 'he has a *powerful* (or *strong*) mind, but it was not then in a *vigorous* state.' A *powerful* style, implies great ability; a *vigorous* style, the exertion of that ability.

'Forcible' is never used to describe qualities of either mind or body, but only the individual efforts which those qualities may call forth; it is *generally* applied to *mental* efforts; we speak of a forcible argument, a forcible illustration; but it is sometimes applied as the adjective corresponding to the noun *force*, implying coercive violence, as 'to make a forcible entry,' &c; the adverb 'forcibly' is also used in this sense. There is, however, a difference between the mental efforts designated as 'strong' and 'forcible.' A 'forcible' expression is one both strong and *to the point.* A 'strong' expression is merely vehement.

'Potent' is occasionally used for reasoning, but generally when speaking of the properties of drugs, poisonous, medicinal, or intoxicating, as 'a potent drug,' a 'potent dram.'

INCONSISTENT, INCONGRUOUS.

'Inconsistent' is almost always applied either to character or conduct, though we sometimes speak of 'two inconsistent opinions or propositions.' But a proposition can only be inconsistent as compared with another proposition; if we speak of an inconsistent opinion, it is always as compared with some other, previously alluded to, or understood as being held by the same person. A man is sometimes taxed with inconsistency, from having changed his opinions; a charge, which, if true, would cause every person to be inconsistent, who was neither foolishly obstinate nor born perfect. The real inconsistency is, not the 'being wiser to-day than we were yesterday,' but the holding at the *same moment* contradictory opinions, or implying by our conduct that we do not hold them.

At first sight it would seem as if consistency in conduct was impossible, since every one who professes to act on principle must more or less fall short of the standard of perfection; and in this sense all mortals are inconsistent. But what is generally regarded as emphatically inconsistent, is not the falling occasionally into faults, but the holding two different standards of action,— *aiming* at one thing and professing another; as when a person professes, in the abstract, a great horror of falsehood, and yet holds that it is allowable to lie on certain occasions, or for certain reasons. One who is at the same time religious and worldly in his conduct, presents the commonest example of this kind of inconsistency. There is a difference between 'serving *two* masters,' and serving *one* from whom we may sometimes stray.

'Incongruous' is generally applied to some *production*,

viewed as a whole, whose parts do not agree with each other. A mixture of architectural styles in one building — a dress which is in part homely, in part elaborate — or a selection of colors which do not harmonize, are all incongruous. Thus the term is applied to all works of art or skill in which this defect is perceived.

CRUEL, BARBAROUS, INHUMAN, SAVAGE.

A 'cruel' man is one who takes pleasure in another's pain. A 'barbarous' man is one who inflicts pain, whether from spite, revenge, or interest, in a wild and violent manner. 'Savage' is much the same as 'barbarous,' but rather an exaggeration of it, implying even more violence.

One who is 'inhuman,' again, is utterly dead to compassion — he may not take delight in *purposely* inflicting suffering; but he either inflicts it if he sees cause, or endures the sight of it, without either compunction or pity: — he is hard-hearted.

SUBLIME, MAGNIFICENT, SPLENDID, GRAND, SUPERB.

'Sublime' is the highest and strongest of these words. When applied to the productions of genius, whether in art or literature, it is always limited to such as are in the loftiest style of excellence — of such kinds as inspire awe rather than delight. In natural scenery it is the same; those landscapes which are called 'sublime' must be characterized by the most awful and lofty character, and it is never applied to anything on a small scale, whether in art or nature.* It also differs from all the other words under consideration, in being applied to human actions and sentiments; heroic conduct, or an elevated tone of feeling or principles of morality, are sometimes called 'sublime.'

---

* See Burke's remarks in the *Essay on the Sublime and Beautiful.*

'Magnificent' is also applied to objects of beauty on a large and grand scale, but it is never properly applied to human conduct, nor to productions of the fine arts, (except architecture,) or of literature. It is only correctly used to qualify — 1st, scenery and natural objects, such as birds and beasts, and even human beings, considered only in reference to their personal and *material* endowments; and, 2dly, those artificial productions which belong rather to the costly, pompous, and luxurious in the artistic class; as buildings, furniture, jewelry, &c. For example, we should not speak correctly of a statue or picture, when considering it in the light of a work of art, as being magnificent, but we might speak of a magnificent palace or set of jewels. On the other hand, we might speak of a beautiful woman, *if on a large scale*, so that the *material* is prominent, as 'magnificent.' We might also call her voice, if possessing much volume and richness of tone, 'magnificent,' but not her style of singing.

Architecture forms an exception to the other fine arts, in this respect; the terms 'magnificent' and 'splendid' may be applied to it; but it does not in reality form an exception to the rule before mentioned; as a simple and grand style of building would never be called 'magnificent;' it is only in so far as its *gorgeous* and *costly* character strikes us that we use that term, as in the rich and complicated florid Gothic architecture.

'Splendid' is like 'magnificent,' but rather less strong in its signification; it differs also in this point, that it is applied to abstract qualities, which 'magnificent' never is; we speak of '*splendid* talents,' 'a *splendid* display of genius,' &c. It always implies something brilliant, gorgeous, or striking.

'Grand' is merely used for something in a great or lofty style.

'Superb' is nearly the same as magnificent, but has been less completely adopted into our language, being still somewhat Frenchified.

PLEASING, AGREEABLE, PLEASANT.

'Pleasing' is generally applied to manners and personal appearance. 'Agreeable' is used in a more extended sense: when applied to manners and conversation it differs from 'pleasing,' and means rather clever and entertaining, than winning or attractive. Many persons are 'agreeable' who are not 'pleasing'; and a 'pleasing' person may not have sufficient spirit, or variety of conversation, to constitute him 'agreeable.' 'Pleasing' refers more to the person himself; 'agreeable' to the impression made on others.

'Pleasant' was formerly used to describe merry and playful conversation, or a jocose and lively person; now it is in a great measure withdrawn from persons and applied to things, — to weather, scenery, situations, &c.

'Pleasantry' is a relic of the old meaning. The French *plaisant* has changed in a reverse way. Formerly it meant what *we now* call 'pleasant,' as may be seen from the 'Lament of Mary Queen of Scots:' —

> 'Adieu, *plaisant* pays de France!'

Now it has come to mean, as it formerly did with us, 'funny' or 'jocose.'

CALM, TRANQUIL, QUIET, PLACID.

'Calm' applies either to the outward manner, to the temperament, or to the mood of mind at the moment. 'Tranquil,' properly speaking, only to the mood of mind. There is also a difference in the state which they describe.

Tranquillity implies not only outward serenity, but ease of mind. If we exhort a person 'to be *calm*,' we are merely advising him to practise self-control: the expression, 'you may be *tranquil*,' implies, 'you need feel no alarm.' A strong-minded person will be *calm* in the midst of dangers and calamities; but if we say, 'He saw his country ruined with a *tranquil* eye,' it would imply, not firmness of soul, but apathy.

'Quiet' is more applicable, in general, to external circumstances than to temper or manner; when applied to these, it implies a silent, retiring disposition.

'Placid' is something like 'tranquil,' but implies less of quiescence, and more of cheerful ease and smoothness. If we speak of 'a *placid* sea,' it implies a more settled state than 'tranquil.' The sea might be both tranquil and gloomy.

DELIGHTFUL, DELICIOUS.

'Delightful' is applied both to the pleasures of the mind and those of the senses: 'delicious' only to those of the senses. An excursion, a social circle, a place of abode, may be 'delightful;' a perfume, or a fruit, 'delicious.' 'Delightful' may be used, however, for all pleasures connected with the bodily senses, except taste; a climate, a breeze, a scent, may be either 'delightful' or 'delicious.' 'Delicious' is limited, in general, to the lower senses — taste, smell, or feeling

Some people do sometimes speak of music as 'delicious;' but they are generally those who regard music chiefly as a sensual pleasure, or what the Germans call an *ohrenschmaus*, or banquet for the ears — something that does not concern the mind. No one possessing a musician's soul ever denominated music as 'a *delicious* art.'

'Delightful' is also applied to moral gratification. A well-ordered and happy family — a joyful reunion — are *delightful* to witness.

OBSTINATE, STUBBORN.

'Both *obstinacy* and *stubbornness* imply an excessive and vicious perseverence in pursuing our own judgment in opposition to that of others; but to be *obstinate* implies the doing what we ourselves chose. To be *stubborn* denotes, rather, not to do what others advise or desire. An *obstinate* man will pursue his own foolish purpose, in spite of the wisest and kindest counsel. A *stubborn* child will not comply with the advice, or obey the commands of a parent. *Obstinacy* requires a positive idea; *stubbornness* merely a negation. *Obstinacy* is generally applied to the superior; *stubbornness* to the inferior. An *obstinate* king, under a false appearance of firmness, brings ruin on his country; a *stubborn* people is insensible to benevolence, and can only be subdued by punishment. *Obstinacy* refers more to outward acts, and *stubbornness* to disposition.' — *Sir J. Mackintosh.*

FICKLE, CAPRICIOUS, VARIABLE, CHANGEABLE.

The first two of these adjectives are, properly speaking, limited to *persons*, and only applied to *things* by a kind of metaphor: the two latter are applied indifferently to persons and things.

The chief difference between 'fickle' and 'capricious' is, that 'fickle' refers rather to a want of *constancy*, whether in tastes or attachments — while 'capricious' not only includes this, but also a disposition to take violent and short-lived fancies or antipathies to persons or things.

A friend whose affection cools speedily is 'fickle;' one who takes sudden and unreasonable likings or dislikes is 'capricious.' In short, 'fickle' conveys the idea of a preference being short-lived; 'capricious' of its being also suddenly formed, and without sufficient cause.

'Variable' and 'changeable' refer for the most part to climate; when applied to persons they preserve an analogy to their original meaning, implying a change rather in the mood of mind than in the affections; a variable temperament is distinguished rather by rapid transitions from grave to gay, from hot to cold, than by actual want of constancy.

'Changeable' is, however, often used to describe that kind of fickleness or caprice, which is also denominated 'whimsicality.'

DEEP, PROFOUND.

'Deep' and 'profound' are often, but not always, synonymous. They differ, first, in this respect — that 'profound' is almost limited to abstract subjects, while 'deep' includes also natural objects. We may speak indifferently of 'a *deep* well,' 'a *deep* color,' or 'a *deep* feeling,' '*deep* learning.' 'Profound' could only be applied in these last cases.

In matters of sentiment and reflection 'deep' is generally, though not uniformly, preferred to 'profound;' in cases in which the particular intellectual faculties are in question, 'profound' is more generally used. We speak of '*deep* sorrow,' '*deep* thought,' — but of '*profound* contempt,' 'a *profound* knowledge of a subject.'

WEIGHTY, HEAVY.

These words bear somewhat the same relation to each other as 'deep' and 'profound.' We speak of 'weighty reasons,' but 'heavy cares.' As a term of blame, 'heavy' is always the word employed; we should say, 'This man's speech contained weighty arguments, but his opponent's was a very *heavy* discourse.'

FAULTLESS, BLAMELESS, SPOTLESS, INNOCENT.

A 'faultless' character is not only free from imputation of evil, but also free from *defects*: one who is blameless or spotless is one whose character has never had any charge brought against it.

Spotless and faultless apply to the general character only; blameless may be used in reference to particular points. We might say, 'He is blameless in this respect'—'in this instance I can declare that I am blameless'—in such phrases we could not use the words 'faultless' or 'spotless.'

'Faultless' may also be applied (which the other two cannot be) to personal appearance as well as mind.

'Innocent' is sometimes used to indicate a state of utter ignorance of evil, like that of a child; at other times it is used in opposition to 'guilt'—to imply that a person is free from the fault with which he is charged. Innocent, in this last sense, (like guilty) is used in reference to *actions* and not feelings or intentions: thus differing from 'spotless' and 'faultless.'

Our first parents were *innocent* till the moment of their tasting of the forbidden tree; but they could not be called 'spotless' or 'faultless,' since as sin evidently lies in the intention, they incurred it as soon as the wish to commit the act had been fully formed. From a want of comprehension of this, and an inattention to the meaning of the word innocent, much confusion of thought is produced. Adam and Eve being often spoken of as if they were not only innocent, but faultless and spotless, before the fall.

WICKED, SINFUL, CRIMINAL, DEPRAVED, GUILTY.

The word 'wicked' affords a curious exemplification of the kind of change, through which words now indicative of evil have frequently passed. It originally meant 'alive,' as 'wick, still does in the north of England. The 'wick' of a candle has the same origin, meaning the living or flaming part of it; and the word 'quick' was the same. From 'alive' and 'lively,' 'wicked' came to signify restless and turbulent, and at last assumed its present sense, expressive of unmitigated moral evil, either of character or actions.

'Criminal' always implies the commission of some fault which is considered as such in the sight of Man; and generally, with reference to human laws, supposed to be *just;* for transgressions of *iniquitous* laws, though in one sense they may be termed *crimes*, are not correctly designated as *criminal.* Under the earlier Roman emperors, the profession of Christianity was punished as a crime: but it would never be described as criminal. The laws to which such actions are ideally referred, must be *supposed*, then, to be just and equitable.

Whatever, in this sense, then, is criminal, must also, be sinful; but 'sinful' designates faults only as they incur the *divine* displeasure; hence the word is far more extended in meaning than 'criminal:' it extends to thoughts and words as well as actions; while 'criminal,' if ever used in reference to thoughts, is only so employed in as far as they are supposed to *lead* to actions.

We occasionally speak of 'a *criminal* thirst for vengeance,' &c., but it is always with reference to this passion as naturally leading to the *crime* of murder; and the conjugate word *crime* is never correctly used except to designate an action; while the word 'sin' may not only refer to a thought, but even quite as frequently to general evil propensities and tendencies.

'Depraved' implies not only positive wickedness, but an entire *corruption* of nature.

One who is depraved must originally have been capable of

something better.* It is extended to character as well as actions.

'Guilty,' like 'criminal,' always has reference to some positive action, and to *human* condemnation ; whereas 'wicked' and 'depraved' may apply to the whole character, as well as to individual acts. But 'guilty' refers chiefly to the question of a person's *having* or *not* having actually *committed* a certain action, while 'criminal' may be considered rather as describing the character of that action. We might say, 'He is *guilty* of such and such a fault; but he is not as *criminal* as some of his companions in so acting.' Guilt does not admit of *degree*, though it does of *amount*. A person may be guilty of more or of less crime, but cannot be more or less guilty in what he *has* committed; though he may be more or less wicked, sinful, or criminal.†

BENEVOLENT, BENEFICENT, CHARITABLE, MUNIFICENT, LIBERAL, BOUNTIFUL, PHILANTHROPIC.

Benevolent and beneficent, together with their conjugates, have curiously diverged from their original meaning. Etymologically, 'benevolent' implied merely *wishing* well to others, and 'beneficent' *doing* well;‡ *now*, 'benevolent' includes both kinds of feelings and actions, and 'beneficent' is restricted to acts of kindness on a great scale, and generally performed by some one of exalted station and character; hence we speak of the 'beneficence' rather than the 'benevolence' of the Creator. It may perhaps be said to follow from this, that 'benevolent' draws our attention more to the character of the agent, 'beneficent,' to that of

---

* It is in this sense that we speak of the *depravity* of human nature. It was a fall from a better state.

† See Archbishop Whately's Charge *on Infant Baptism.*

‡ The French use the corresponding words 'bienveillance' and 'bienfaisance' more correctly according to their etymology.

the act performed; retaining, so far, a tinge of their etymology.

'Charitable' (when not used in reference to a mild and candid judgment of others) seems to be restricted to one kind of benevolence, that which consists in almsgiving.

'Munificent' resembles 'beneficent,' in referring always to favors on a large scale, and conferred by superiors; but there is this important difference, that 'beneficent' always implies some real and essential good done, while 'munificent' (as its derivation implies) may be applied equally to any *gift*, whether really useful or not.* One who makes a present of jewelry or pictures to a friend is munificent, but would not be called 'beneficent.' If he raised a distressed family from starvation, the word 'beneficent' would be more appropriate. But one who gives largely to the Public, or to some institution, is called munificent. It seems to convey the idea of splendor; no one can be called munificent who does not give on a large scale.

Any one who is ready to give *freely*, as the etymology implies, on whatever scale, is 'liberal.' 'Bountiful,' again, is stronger than 'liberal,' and implies giving in abundance; it also differs from 'liberal,' in being restricted to *giving;* while 'liberal' is applied to any easy style of expenditure in general; to the reverse, in short, of 'stingy,' or 'miserly.' Many people live in a *liberal* style, who are very far from being 'bountiful.' Bountiful always seems to imply, giving out of an ample store.

'Philanthropic' (as its etymology indicates) implies benevolence solely in reference to the *human race* — and always to masses, not to individuals. One who devises some plan to benefit numbers is called 'philanthropic'; but we should

* 'Munificent' nearly answers to the Greek word *megaloprepes*, as described by Aristotle.

not talk of 'philanthropically giving a loaf to a hungry child.' — (See note to Preface.)

BENIGNANT, KIND, GOOD-NATURED.

'Benignant' is an expression more generally used to describe manner than actions; and almost always refers to the manners of a superior. It seems to imply a condescending amenity of deportment. 'Kind' is used to describe both manners and conduct, and has by far the most extended signification of the three words: it includes almost every manifestation of benevolence, small or great. 'Good-natured,' on the other hand, is limited to its lowest exercise, to kindness in trifles, and always to kindness springing from constitutional obligingness and amiability. A person who is kind from conscientiousness alone, is never called 'good-natured.'

The old original word was '*well*-natured,' which is grammatically more correct than the modern word; for the adverb is properly used to qualify the adjective. We speak of 'well-born,' 'well-bred,' not of 'good-born,' &c. A person of a good disposition is said to be *well*-disposed, not *good*-disposed. In old English, the word '*well*-tempered' was used instead of '*good*-tempered.'

NEGLECTFUL, NEGLIGENT.

'Neglectful' has reference generally to our conduct towards *persons;* 'negligent' towards *things*. A person is said to be neglectful of his friends; negligent of his business. A *negligent* correspondent is one who is careless in writing, mislays letters, and forgets whether he has answered them or no; a *neglectful* correspondent is one who forgets his friends when away from them, and acts on the maxim — 'Out of sight, out of mind.'

Hence, if we reproach a person with *neglect* (the substantives 'neglect' and 'negligence' correspond with the adjectives), we are supposed to charge him with real unkindness or coldness; while only carelessness is implied if he is charged with negligence.

The verb 'to neglect' is a conjugate of both these adjectives and substantives. We might say, 'He did not use to neglect his business, but he has been very *negligent* of it lately;' 'I did not think he would neglect his friends, but he has been very *neglectful* of me.'

ABSENT, ABSTRACTED.

'Absent' refers merely to the circumstance of the attention being withdrawn from outward objects; 'abstracted' implies also concentration of the thoughts on something foreign to what is before us. One who is 'absent' does not attend to what is around him — it may be from languor of mind or carelessness; but one who is 'abstracted' is inattentive because he is thinking of something else. 'Absence' is therefore a habit; 'abstraction' an accident. We do sometimes, indeed, speak of an habitually absent person as 'abstracted;' but one who is from any particular cause in an abstracted state of mind would not be called an 'absent' person. Byron's *Dying Gladiator*, who

> 'Heard it, but he heeded not; his thoughts
> Were with his heart, and that was far away,'

was then *abstracted;* but to call him *absent* would be ludicrous.

TRIFLING, TRIVIAL.

A *trifling* matter is one merely of small importance: a *trivial* matter is a small matter made too much of. The word 'trivial' implies contempt, which 'trifling' does not. By saying, 'He never neglects a *trifling* matter,' we are rather supposed to praise; but in blaming a person for frivolity, we often say, 'He is always engrossed with *trivial* concerns.' The substantive 'trifle' is conjugate to both.

FATHERLY, PATERNAL; MOTHERLY, MATERNAL; BROTHERLY, FRATERNAL; KINGLY, REGAL.

These pairs of words are formed from corresponding roots in Latin and Saxon; and, as has been already observed, they all bear nearly the same relation to each other; the Latin word being the more polite and cold, the Saxon the more hearty and cordial. In these groups of words, also, the Latin word is always used to express the *office*, the Saxon the manners and deportment. We speak of 'a *paternal* government'—'*maternal* duties;' but of 'a *fatherly* kindness of manner'—'a *motherly* tenderness.' The same may be said of the relation between the words 'kingly' and 'regal.' We speak of the 'regal state'—'the regal prerogative'—but of a '*kingly* deportment'—'kingly splendor.'

FRIENDLY, AMICABLE.

The same relation exists between these two words; neither denote any strong affection, neither are conjugate to the noun 'friendship;' but 'friendly' implies something of real cordiality, while 'amicable' hardly signifies more than that the persons specified are not disposed to quarrel; thence we speak of '*amicable* relations between foreign States.'

RIGHTEOUS, JUST.

We have here again a Saxon * and a Latin term, whose roots exactly correspond in meaning; but they have even more curiously diverged than many other pairs of words.

* The root of the word 'righteous' is, in fact, both Latin and Saxon, the words 'recht' and 'rectus' being evidently of kindred origin.

'Righteous' is now exclusively applied to rectitude of conduct drawn from *religious* principle, while 'just' is simply used for moral uprightness. A heathen or atheist may be called *just*, but not *righteous*. But many are apt to overlook the fact, that these words were really and originally the same. For instance, in the Douay version of the Bible, made from the Vulgate, the words of Latin derivation are invariably preferred to the Saxon; and we find 'just' constantly used for 'righteous,' as the translation of the Greek *dikaios*.

CALCULATED, FIT, SUITABLE, APT.

'Calculated' is always so employed as not to lose the force of the figure. It must be read with an emphasis, and followed by words which direct and qualify its meaning, or explain its application; as 'These plants are *calculated* for our climate.'

'Suitable,' and 'fit,' may be used by themselves, which could not be the case with 'calculated.' We might say indifferently — 'Do you think him calculated — fit — or suitable, for this situation?' but we might also say more briefly, 'Do you think him suitable or fit?' in this last case, 'calculated' would be inadmissible. 'Calculated' must also be differently qualified: we speak of 'very fit' — but of 'very *well* calculated.'

'Apt' is somewhat different from the others. It rather implies readiness than suitability: and it is used to qualify a simile or illustration; in which sense it implies not only 'suitable' but 'happy' — or 'pointed.' It is also used in the sense of 'liable,' as, 'I am very *apt* to forget.'

ACCURATE, EXACT, PRECISE.

What is accurate must be exact; but exactness does not necessarily imply accuracy. An account of any transaction may be *accidentally* exact, but to be accurate, care must have been bestowed. An *accurate* writer is one who *aims* at exactness.

We speak of an 'exact coincidence,'—we should not use the word 'accurate' in this sense. 'Precise,' when applied to *things*, is nearly the same as 'exact,' but less extended in signification. A likeness may be exact, but could not be precise. It is most correctly applied to anything which is within certain defined limits, thus adhering to its etymology, which signifies, 'cut to a pattern,' (from the Latin *præ-cido.*)

It is curious that the expression, 'an exact person,' is synonymous with 'an *accurate* person;' but 'a *precise* person' always implies one who is over-strict and scrupulous in trifles.

FAMOUS, CELEBRATED, ILLUSTRIOUS, RENOWNED.

Famous and celebrated approach the nearest to each other in meaning of this group; but 'famous' seems to convey the idea of a name being more 'blazoned abroad,' and loudly praised, than 'celebrated.' 'Illustrious' always implies fame of a lofty and elevated character. We may speak of 'a famous juggler,' 'a celebrated chess-player,' but we should not call them illustrious. 'Illustrious' is also used for distinguished rank and station.

'Renowned' resembles 'famous,' but, like illustrious, is used for a high and dignified kind of reputation. 'A renowned chess-player' could be so called only in irony.

SLY, CUNNING, CRAFTY, DECEITFUL.

'Sly' differs from 'cunning' and 'crafty,' first, by indicating manifestations of deceit on a *small scale*, and, secondly, from its being generally of a *negative* character, implying rather concealment than invention. We speak of '*sly* humor;' this seems to imply humor that is furtive and covert, in opposition to '*broad* humor.'

'Cunning' has departed, in some degree, from its original meaning, 'knowing' (from a word cognate with the German *kennen*, to know,) and now implies deceit, united with a *low* kind of skill or cleverness.

'Crafty' (according to its etymology) implies some higher degree of mental power, united with deceit. A statesman is called crafty; a fortune-teller cunning; a child sly.

'Deceitful' differs from these in applying more to *character* than to individual acts; while the three other words would equally suit both. It may also (like the substantive 'deception,' which is in fact its real conjugate) be applied to illusory appearances.

We might say 'these appearances are *deceitful;* the cause of the *deception* is so and so.' — (See the head DECEIT, DECEPTION.)

NOUNS.

DILIGENCE, INDUSTRY.

'Industry' *includes* 'diligence;' but it includes also something more. An industrious* man not only labors perseveringly at any given task, but is constantly on the watch for opportunities to improve his condition or his mind, as the case may be. The term is therefore applied to the *design*, as well as to the execution. The industrious man is always ready for employment—always looking out for fresh work. The diligent man merely performs steadily *the individual task* he may be set. No one could be called industrious who was not also diligent in the execution of his task; but if we set a child some lesson to learn, we do not usually exhort him to 'industry,' but to 'diligence.' They are often, however, used synonymously.

CONTENTMENT, SATISFACTION.

'Contentment' may be classed among those words in the English language which adhere strictly to their etymology. Its root was undoubtedly the verb 'to contain,' and the substantive and its adjective have not departed from this meaning. A contented person does not indulge in fruitless wishes for what is beyond his reach; his desires are limited by what he possesses.

'Satisfaction' implies more: this word has likewise retained the signification of its root, and means that we have

---

* The nouns and adjectives here correspond.

obtained all we want; not that our desires are *limited*, but that they have been *gratified*. A poor and needy man may be 'contented,' but he cannot feel 'satisfaction' with his condition. We might say, 'Since I cannot obtain *satisfaction*, I must be *content* without it.

'Satisfaction' also implies an *amende honorable*. Sometimes, when applied to conduct, it indicates approbation — as, 'Your behavior gives me great *satisfaction*.' 'Satisfied' implies a less amount of gratification: 'I am *satisfied* with your conduct,' implies less of praise than 'It gives me *satisfaction*.'

'*Not content*' and '*not satisfied*' differ in this in modern usage, that the latter often signifies not being pleased *at all*, which the former does not in English, though it does in French. The Pope was not *satisfied* with the Reformation of Henry VIII.; but the reformers were not *content* with it.

ANGER, INDIGNATION, DISPLEASURE, RESENTMENT.

The difference between 'anger' and 'indignation' is, that 'anger' is always *personal*, and always applies to injuries inflicted, or supposed to be inflicted, on ourselves, or on others so nearly connected by ties of kindred or friendship, as to be regarded almost as a part of ourselves.

'Indignation' is more generally used in reference to some injustice or oppression shown to others, whether to strangers or friends; though it also includes anger on our own account. It may be considered as denoting *sympathetic anger*; — a feeling that such and such conduct *might justly* provoke anger. And hence it is that a person, under the influence of *anger* at some wrong done him, often prefers describing himself as feeling 'indignation;' meaning thereby to disavow selfish *personal* feelings, and to imply that he is affected merely by the character of the act *in itself*, just as he would have been, had the wrong been done to a stranger.

'Displeasure' is a calmer feeling than either 'anger' or 'indignation.' It implies a sentiment scarcely stronger than simple disapproval, and is generally applied to the faults of an inferior, either in age or station. We should not speak of being 'displeased' at the conduct of a superior, however ill we might think of him.

'Resentment' is a stronger feeling than any of those before mentioned. It generally implies a *long-continued* feeling. It may be defined as a long-continued anger felt against some one who has *knowingly injured us;* in no other case can the word be correctly applied.

We may feel 'anger' against a child for behaving ill, though his conduct may do us no harm; we may be angry with some one who is the innocent cause of annoyance to us; but in neither of these cases should we be said to feel 'resentment.'

RECOMPENSE, REWARD, MEED.

A 'recompense' implies a reward equivalent to the action done (etymologically, a *compensation*).

A 'reward' *includes* a recompense, but does not *imply* it —its simple, primary meaning is merely a pleasure or benefit (whether adequate or not) conferred in return for some action. We may say: 'I cannot *recompense* you for this;' meaning, 'I cannot make any fitting return to you.' Hence it is incorrect to speak of *recompensing* a child for good behavior; 'reward' would be the correct term. 'Meed' is a reward which we *earn* by our own exertions, and to which we are fairly entitled: A *free gift* cannot be a *meed.*

APPROVAL, APPROBATION.

'Approbation' is used in a much more extended sense than 'approval.' 'Approval generally implies a formal sanction of some plan or mode of action; as, 'I proposed such a measure to the Prime Minister, for his *approval.*' It implies also such a sanction as can only come from *a superior ;* whereas, 'approbation' requires no such distinctions. A private man may give his 'approbation' to the measures of government; but we could not say that he gave them his 'approval.'

Lastly, some *consequences* must follow *for* an 'approval;' while 'approbation' does not necessarily imply anything of the kind.

TIMIDITY, BASHFULNESS, SHYNESS, DIFFIDENCE.

'Timidity' implies a liability to fear of any kind, whether personal or moral. 'Bashfulness,' 'shyness,' and 'diffidence,' all refer to the fear of blame or disapprobation. But a person may be shy or bashful without being diffident. 'Diffidence' implies a real distrust of our own powers, combined with a fear lest our failure should be censured; for a dread of failure unconnected with censure is not usually called 'diffidence.' We should not say that Robinson Crusoe on his island, if he distrusted his own powers of building a canoe, was *diffident.* The word seems to imply spectators, and the companionship of others. It is generally applied to a reluctance to attempt some undertaking, or a fear of exhibiting our own powers; but 'shyness' and 'bashfulness' are more applicable to general deportment and manners.

'Bashfulness' is generally applied to an awkward, sheepish kind of 'timidity;' 'shyness' to an excessive self-consciousness, and a continual impression that every one is looking at us. Bashfulness would be shown by hanging back timidly, or sitting silent and stupefied. Shyness is often manifested by an apparent haughtiness and stateliness of manner, (hence it is almost proverbially mistaken for pride,) or, still oftener, by an affected smile, and a frequent forced laugh.

In short, 'shyness' invariably arises from thinking too much about oneself, 'diffidence' generally from underrating one's own powers, (which is compatible with perfect self-possession,) and 'bashfulness' and 'timidity' from a fearful disposition and a want of presence of mind. Shyness and bashfulness, however, imply *awkwardness*, which timidity does not.

SORROW, GRIEF, AFFLICTION, DISTRESS, REGRET, SADNESS, MELANCHOLY.

'Sorrow' and 'affliction' are used generally — 'grief' only for particular cases. We speak of 'such an one having known *sorrow*' or 'affliction,' but not of 'having known *grief*.' 'Grief' is usually applied to 'sorrow' for some definite causes, and always for *the past*. We speak of feeling 'grief' for the *death* of a friend, but not for his illness or misconduct at this present moment. In such a case, 'sorrow' or 'affliction' would be better words.

'Sorrow' and 'grief' always imply *mental* distress; 'affliction' is used in a more extended sense, and is sometimes applied to one class of bodily evils, — to those, namely, which are occasioned by the privation of a sense, or the loss of a bodily power. Pain and sickness, however severe, are not called *afflictions*, though a person suffering from them may be said to be *afflicted;* but blindness, deafness, or loss of the use of any of the limbs, are constantly spoken of as 'afflictions.'

'Distress' may be used either generally, or particularly.

It includes a wider range of evils than affliction, — for poverty, sickness, and pain, come under this head. When applied in particular to any one kind of evil, it usually expresses an uneasy, restless suffering, whether of body or mind — or else very pressing, griping poverty ; — and it almost always implies a struggle. One who is sunk in despair would not be said to be in 'distress.'

'Sadness' and 'melancholy' are both applied to moods of the mind exclusively.

'Regret' is used for a slighter kind of sorrow than any of the words above mentioned ; when used in speaking of losses by death, it implies the mildest degree of sorrow. In its stronger sense, it is chiefly used when speaking of our past conduct, and in this case its meaning is very limited. We feel remorse or repentance for deep and heavy faults, 'regret' only for follies or carelessness. But 'regret' has a special reference to one particular kind of repentance — that which is felt for having *lost an opportunity.*

Conjugate words. — 'Grief' was formerly used in the sense of the French 'grief,' for a subject of complaint or injury. It has preserved this sense in two of its pseudo-paronymes, or conjugates — 'to aggrieve' and 'grievance.' 'Grievous' was formerly used for an illness or accident, where we now say 'severe,' and now is used to qualify an event at which we feel 'sorrow' mingled with a degree of *vexation.* *Grieved* is a far less strong expression than 'grief.' We say to a child who has behaved ill, — 'I am *grieved* at your conduct,' but we should not speak of being *in grief* for such a cause.

'Sorry,' again, is a much weaker expression than 'sorrow.' The description once given by a foreigner of the grief of some friends of his for the loss of their only child — 'They are *very sorry,*' would almost raise a laugh in England ; and yet in old English, as we see by our Bible translation, 'sorry' was regarded as answering to 'sorrow.' 'And when his fellow-servants heard that, they were very sorry.'

'Afflicted' has a double meaning. It is used for 'being *visited* with affliction,' or, for the state of mind naturally produced by it — the state of 'grief' or 'sorrow.' This last meaning is applied by metonymy, just as the adjective 'melancholy' was formerly used for a sad disposition, and now for incidents or speeches which may *occasion* 'sadness.' *Sad* has also acquired this secondary meaning. This word has undergone some curious changes. Being derived from the verb *to sit*, it was formerly used very much in the sense of *settled*, as now applied to conduct; indeed, in old times it signified *firm*, as in Wickliffe's translation of the Bible, where the 'house built upon a *rock*,' is said to be built upon a *sad* stone. Hence it came to signify seriousness, both of character and of material objects; thus *sad garments*, for what the French called *un habit serieux*. Its meaning at present, as well as that of the noun, still verges upon the idea of earnestness, as in the rather old-fashioned expression, 'in *sober sadness*,' — that is, 'in *collected earnestness*.'

FEAR, FRIGHT, TERROR, ALARM, DREAD, APPREHENSION.

'Fear' is a general term, which includes many of the rest. It is sometimes spoken of as a *passion*; sometimes as a mere intellectual consciousness of danger. It is also used, as far as this latter is concerned, in two senses: 1st, the apprehension of *actual* danger; 2dly, the *hypothetical* apprehension. For instance, 'I have a great *fear* of catching cold,' implies the *actual* apprehension of an evil — *i. e.*, 'catching cold;' but 'I have a great *fear* of being out in the rain,' implies a *hypothetical* apprehension. What is understood by it is, 'I have a *fear* of the evil *which may be produced* by going out in the rain — viz., catching cold.*

'Fright' implies a degree of fear which paralyzes and takes complete possession of the mind. 'Terror' is the same thing in a stronger degree. 'Alarm' merely signifies a *sudden* apprehension of immediately-impending danger, probably derived from the Italian '*All' armi!*' a common cry of soldiers when surprised. A brave man may be 'alarmed,' (for it implies nothing unreasonable or cowardly in its primary sense,) and he may feel 'fear;' but he could not be 'frightened.'

'Dread' differs from 'fear' in being more *definite* and more *intense:* we may speak of 'being *in a state* of *fear*' without reference to the object feared; but not, of 'being in a state of *dread*.'†

'Fear,' 'fright,' and 'alarm' are, in general, only used for apprehension of some painful or destructive physical evil; the two last constantly: but 'fear' is often used in reference to the opinion of others, especially those whom we respect. Men are said to be 'governed by the *fear* of the world, the *fear* of their superiors,' &c.; and 'fear' has always been the most appropriate expression that is used in reference to our Creator.

The conjugate verbs, 'to fear' and 'to dread,' do not exactly correspond with the nouns. 'To fear' is generally used for a *hypothetical* apprehension; and 'to dread' is mostly applied in reference to some *impending* evil. The expression, 'I *dread* crossing the sea,' would imply that we

---

* The adjective 'afraid' has the same varieties of meaning. It may be said to be conjugate to the noun 'fear.' 'To be afraid,' however, when used alone, means nearly the same as 'to be frightened.'

† 'Dread' was formerly used more as 'fear' is now. It was used towards the Deity, as we may see in our liturgy.

expected *soon* to cross. 'To dread' may also be applied to any evil, whether connected with positive pain or danger, or not. 'I *dread* the meeting with such an one,' might be used by one who expected to be afflicted with sorrow or agitation at the meeting, 'I *fear* meeting him,' would imply that the meeting would be the cause of some physical evil or danger. We should not say, 'I *fear* committing a crime,' unless we meant that we feared the *punishment* the crime might bring on us; if our fear was based on conscientious or honorable motives, we should use the word 'dread.'* With regard to the faults of *others*, however, we say 'fear:' I *fear* he may be led into such and such an action.'

'Apprehension' simply implies the consciousness of danger. It is a word which has undergone some change in its meaning. Originally, it was used merely to express *expectation*, or simple consciousness, without implying necessarily the expectation of consciousness of *danger;* and this original sense has been preserved in its derivative or conjugate verb, 'to apprehend.' By degrees, the idea of fear or danger came to be understood in the case of the noun substantive, and also the adjective, 'apprehensive.'

The conjugates belonging to this group have most of them preserved their original meaning; but 'fearful' may either be applied to one who feels fear, or to circumstances calculated to inspire the feeling. And 'frightful,' which is now limited in its meaning to that which is likely to *inspire fright*, was formerly used in speaking of *persons* who were easily frightened. This change of expression by metonymy has taken place with many words in our language.

---

* The expression 'to be afraid,' conveys the same idea as 'dread,' with respect to committing a fault. A brave and conscientious person will be 'afraid' of nothing so much as of doing wrong.

PATIENCE, FORTITUDE, RESIGNATION.

'Fortitude' may be classed in two ways: it may either be reckoned with courage, intrepidity, &c., on the one hand, or with 'patience' and 'resignation on the other. It may be called a *link* between two classes of virtues. It is always used, however, in the same sense; as, a *rssistance* to evil rather than a *submission* to it; it is shown in sustaining firmly some violent and overwhelming shock, whether bodily or mental. 'Patience,' on the other hand, implies a gentle submission to the lesser evils of life, and an endurance of *continuous* suffering, whether of body or mind.

'Fortitude' would be shown in sustaining some great calamity or sudden reverse of fortune, or in enduring a severe operation without a groan.

'Patience' is manifested rather in bearing a lingering illness with serenity and gentleness — in enduring some continuous and wearying, though not violent pain — or trials from the bad temper or ill conduct of others. It is also applied to unremitting perseverance in some disagreeable or discouraging task or duty. A person is spoken of as being a *patient* teacher of stupid or inattentive pupils — as not losing 'patience' when trying to conquer some difficulty. In this sense, 'patience' is active; but 'fortitude' is always passive.

The opposite of 'fortitude' is the weakness which yields and is conquered by circumstances: a want of it is manifested by giving way to uncontrolled grief, terror, or outward expressions of pain. The opposite of 'patience,' on the other hand, is irritability, querulousness, or peevishness. Both are equally necessary, but 'patience' is more frequently so than 'fortitude.' The common evils of life should be submitted to; the greater and rarer ones require to be met with resolution.

'Resignation' more nearly resembles 'patience' than 'fortitude,' inasmuch as it implies submission, and not resistance; but, on the other hand, it is always passive. It is generally applied either to those *mental* evils commonly called *afflictions*, or to *bodily* evils, which, being of a nearly hopeless character, are also classed under the same head. A person is not said to be *resigned* under a violent toothache; but under hopeless blindness, or incurable illness, the term would be properly applied. It therefore refers more to the *mental* suffering which accompanies these evils than to the evils themselves; and, in particular, it implies a readiness to *resign hope*. 'Resignation' always implies a *religious* submission; in this, it differs from the two words before mentioned. A stoic might display fortitude; patience is often the result of a sluggish tameness of character; but nothing short of Christian principle can inspire resignation; its essential character is submission to the will of our Maker.

UTILITY, USEFULNESS.

'Utility' is employed in a more *general* and *abstract* sense than 'usefulness.' We speak of the 'utility' of an invention or discovery; of the 'usefulness' of the article discovered or invented: of the 'utility' of a society or institution; of the 'usefulness' of an individual. 'Usefulness,' however, is sometimes employed in the sense of 'utility;' 'utility' much seldomer in the sense of 'usefulness.' The abstract quality is always called 'utility.' 'Beauty and utility,' for example, are placed in opposition to each other.

EXPENSE, COST.

Strictly speaking, 'expense' should be applied to the purchaser, and 'cost' to the thing purchased. A splendid carriage is a *costly* article; the person who bought it is an *expensive* liver, or one of *expensive* habits. But the original meaning of these words (both adjectives and nouns) has been so corrupted, that they are now used almost indiscriminately one for the other. Still, 'expensive' is generally and most correctly used with reference to the means of the purchaser; and 'costly' with reference to the value of the article bought. Many persons are tempted to buy articles of dress or furniture because they are not *costly*, forgetting that, if their means are small, these purchases may still be too *expensive;* and, generally speaking, there are few ways in which more 'expense' is incurred than in constantly buying what are called 'great bargains.'

WISDOM, PRUDENCE.

'Wisdom,' in the words of one writer,* 'consists in the ready and accurate perception of analogies:' and in those of another, 'in the employment of the best means for the attainment of the most important ends:' the one being the description of the *faculty*, the other of its *operation.*

'Prudence' is a lower kind of 'wisdom:' it consists in the employment of the best means for the accomplishment of *any* one particular end, whether it be important or no. A man may therefore be prudent in some things and not in others; for example, if his careful and diligent pursuit of riches should peril his soul. Prudence, again, is of a more *negative* character than wisdom: it rather consists in avoiding danger than in taking a decided step for the accomplishment of any object. A *prudent* general is one who will not let himself be surprised or taken at disadvantage; but not always one who gains victories. A *prudent* statesman will keep out of war and debt, but will not always pass

---

* See Archbishop Whately's *Rhetoric.*

important laws or make improvemeuts. He may not even show foresight in respect of very *distant* evils. Sir Robert Walpole appears to have been a *prudent* statesman for *his own* day; but he showed a want of real wisdom in taking no measures to allay the irritation which existed in the Highlands, and which, though it did not break out in *his* time, was a source of great evils a few years afterwards.*

'Prudence,' in short, takes a lower range than 'wisdom.' The Greeks had only one word for both, *phronimos*. The word *sophos* is sometimes translated 'wise,' but incorrectly: it meant rather 'skilful in the arts;' and, used as a general term, answered to what we call *philosophical*.

SELF-CONCEIT, PRIDE, VANITY, ARROGANCE, HAUGHTINESS.

To be 'self-conceited,' is to entertain an overweening opinion of oneself. A person, however, may be conceited in some things and not in others; he may greatly overrate his own capacity in some *one* particular point, while in others he has a just estimate, or even perhaps too low an estimate of himself.

'Pride,' on the other hand, may be defined as a disposition to rate one's own claims to respect or attention too highly, and to disdain others — viewing our equals as our inferiors, and our superiors as our equals. A proud man, in short, rates very highly what he himself *really possesses* — a self-conceited man *imagines* himself to possess what he really does *not*. And so, the term 'pride of birth,' 'pride of wealth or rank,' &c., means, rating the *claims* of birth or rank very highly. Hence we may see men of high rank and great wealth who look down on those who are far superior in mind to themselves; this does not proceed from their overrating their own abilities, but merely from their

---

* See Macaulay's *Essays*.

overrating the claims of that very wealth and rank, and thinking it entitled to more respect and veneration than the greatest talents or the most eminent virtues.

'Haughtiness' proceeds from pride, but is applied *almost* exclusively to manners and deportment. A *proud* disposition will often show itself in *haughty* manners.

'Vanity' may exist along with pride or self-conceit, but is not implied by either of them. It is a word which has undergone a great variety of changes. Originally it meant emptiness, hollowness, (from the Latin *vanus*,) thence it came to signify something unreal, fictitious, false. This was its meaning in Shakspeare's time; he speaks of 'lying *vainness*.' By degrees its meaning was modified, till it came to be used in the sense which it has now acquired—an excessive desire of applause and approbation for qualities we *do* possess, as well as for those we do not. Persons are said to be vain of their talents or beauty, when they *really* possess these qualifications.

Many extremely vain persons nevertheless underrate themselves; indeed, a high opinion of oneself acts rather as a check than an an incentive to vanity.

'Arrogance' is often confounded with self-conceit, though totally different from it. The quality is, in fact, consistent with a very low opinion of oneself, and a high admiration and respect for others. It has been defined * as 'an habitual and exclusive *self-deference*.' An arrogant man is without deference, even for those of whom *he himself* thinks most highly. He may say, and think, that he is extremely inferior to certain persons; he may hold them in the highest esteem and admiration, but were they to differ from him on any point, even in a matter in which they were fully con-

* See Archbishop Whately's *Rhetoric*, 7th edit. p. 119. See also the article in this work under the head DEFERENCE, &c.

versant and he wholly ignorant, he would set their opinions utterly at nought. He may not have a high estimation of his own powers in general; but practically, on each particular occasion, he appears to consider himself infallible: and this is what leads many to attribute to self-conceit what in reality springs from arrogance.

EFFECTS, CONSEQUENCES, RESULTS.

'Effects' are the *genus*,—'consequences and 'results' the *species*,—therefore 'consequences' and results' must also be 'effects,'—since the species includes the genus,—but 'effects' are not necessarily 'consequences' or 'results.' 'Effects,' as distinguished from the other terms we have mentioned, are applied to something which *immediately* follows from any cause, whether mental or physical. They can therefore be to a certain extent calculated on beforehand. 'Consequences' are more remote and spring less directly from causes; they rather follow in the train of an event. We may *foresee* the 'consequences' of any thing, but we always *act with a view to its* 'effects.' For instance, the effect of wearing clothes, is to cover one; the consequence is, that they wear out; we foresee this *consequence* in buying them, but it is with a view to the immediate *effect* (the covering us) that we act.

Again, we should say, 'His conduct had a bad *effect* on those around him;' but not 'bad *consequences*,' although we might add, 'that the *consequence* of this conduct was,—such and such an event.' Hence we see how much more remote are 'consequences' than 'effects,' simply so called, although a 'consequence' *must be* an 'effect,' as before stated. 'Effects' likewise often imply some direct agency or design, which 'consequences' never do.

'Results' are still more remote than 'consequences.'

'Consequences' and 'effects' are both applied to a change which is in the act of taking place, while 'result' implies the state of things when the change *has* taken place. Hence, it is both more remote and more general than either 'consequences' or 'effects.' We should say, 'My entreaties produced a powerful *effect* on him, and the *result* was that he granted my request.' The 'effect' of ploughing is, the loosening of the soil; the 'consequences' are that seed can be sown on it; the 'result' is, the fertility of the land.

CONFLICT, COMBAT, CONTEST, CONTENTION.

Formerly, the first two of these terms were applied to the striving together of foes in battle; now, 'combat' is the only one used in this sense, though it is sometimes also applied figuratively to the strife of words, or of mental and moral feelings and emotions. But 'conflict' has almost entirely lost its original meaning of a battle or skirmish, and is only applied to it figuratively. A 'contest' was never used for fighting. 'Contest' is generally used for a hot argument or verbal dispute. A 'conflict' is now more frequently applied to an inward struggle of the mind, — to the strife of contending opinions or feelings. We speak of 'undergoing a mental *conflict*' — 'of *conflicting* passions,' &c.; but it is sometimes, though more rarely, used in the sense of 'contest.'

'Contention' was formerly used in the same sense as 'contest' as in Acts, xv. 39 : — 'and the *contention* was so sharp between them,' &c. *Now*, 'contest' is used for the *act* of disputing or quarrelling, and 'contention' for the *habit*. We speak of 'a spirit of *contention*,' (meaning a tendency to *habitual* striving and disputing,) or of 'a contentious disposition;' but never of a 'spirit of contest.'

DETESTATION, AVERSION, ANTIPATHY, DISLIKE, ABHORRENCE, HATRED, REPUGNANCE.

'Aversion' is merely a stronger form of 'dislike;' they differ only in degree, not in kind. We have a dislike to what is unpleasant to us — we have an aversion to something that shocks, disgusts, or inspires us with horror.

'Antipathy' is always used for a *causeless* 'dislike,' or rather for one of which *we cannot define* the cause. Many persons have an 'antipathy' to a cat; this is perhaps not utterly without cause, and may be accounted for by the electricity which resides in that animal; but being without any certain and obvious reason, and unaccountable even to the person who feels it, it is denominated an 'antipathy.'*

'Repugnance' is a feeling akin to disgust; but it is often applied to an extreme reluctance, or shrinking from some particular course of *action*.

'Hatred implies enmity, or a desire for the destruction of its object. It is generally applied to qualities of a personal *kind*, though not always *strictly personal*. It may be directed against abstractions of qualities; as, for instance, we may hate a liar, a traitor, an ungrateful man, in the abstract; but it is rarely directed — perhaps *never* correctly — against qualities belonging to *things*, whether in the abstract or otherwise. In this respect it differs from some of the other words classified here.†

---

* When the discoveries of science shall have thrown more light on the subject, an explanation will, doubtless, be afforded of many at present unaccountable antipathies, both with regard to persons and things.

† Aristotle, in his *Rhetoric*, has given an admirable parallel between 'anger' and 'hatred;' in which he points out that 'anger' can only be directed against an individual or individuals, while 'hatred' may be felt towards a class or nation; that 'anger' only

'Detestation' is somewhat like 'aversion,' but is oftener applied to persons or personal qualities in the abstract. We talk of 'detesting' cruelty or lying — we should not speak of having an 'aversion' to them — because 'aversion' is scarcely ever applied to qualities *in the abstract.*

'Abhorrence' is as strong a term as 'aversion,' but it is differently applied. 'Aversion' may be felt either towards individual *persons* or *things*, but never towards *actions*. 'Abhorrence' is applied generally in reference to *actions*. The proper object of abhorrence is guilt or crime; we may speak, indeed, of our 'abhorrence' of such and such a man; but it is always applied to him as the author of some criminal action, and, strictly speaking, it applies only to bad conduct.

ENEMY, ANTAGONIST, ADVERSARY, OPPONENT.

Of these four words, 'enemy' is the only one which implies general personal hostility. We may be adversaries, antagonists, or opponents of those with whom we are in general on friendly terms. The chief difference, indeed, between an 'enemy' and an 'adversary' is, that the word 'enemy' is oftener applied to one who is personally hostile, and 'adversary' to one who happens for a time to be placed in the *position* of an 'enemy,' as in war or in argument. 'Antagonist' and 'opponent' are generally used in speaking of a single combat, or a debate or dispute between *two*.

---

seeks retaliation, which shall be known and understood as such by its object, while 'hatred' desires destruction; and lastly, that 'anger' cannot subsist at the same moment with 'fear' though 'hatred' and 'fear' are quite compatible. His example, however, has not been followed in this work, in classing 'anger' and 'hatred' together, because, though the two *passions* may often be confounded together, and mistaken one for the other, the two *words* are not liable to be mistaken; and it is with words that we have now to do.

'Antagonist' (as its etymology implies) is applied to one who is *actively struggling* with another, whether literally or in argument. 'Opponent' simply denotes one who differs, or who opposes a *passive* resistance. 'Antagonist' may be used either for real fighting, or for *verbal* disputes; 'opponent,' almost exclusively for the last.

Of these four words, two, 'antagonist' and 'adversary' are exclusively personal. The first, 'enemy,' may be used for one who has a hatred and utter dislike of certain *things;* as, an 'enemy to luxury'—'an enemy to such and such a course.' 'Opponent' is sometimes also used in the same way; we may speak of 'an opponent of such and such measures,' but always *particularly* and never *generally,*—we could not speak, for instance, of an *opponent* to luxury or avarice.

REPROOF, REBUKE, REPRIMAND, CENSURE, REMONSRANCE, EXPOSTULATION, REPROACH.

A 'reproof' is a simple admonition, expressive of our disapprobation, generally addressed to some one beneath us in age or station. 'Rebuke' is now used nearly in the same sense, but is a stronger term. It was formerly applied rather as a 'remonstrance' to an equal, or even to a superior; as in the Bible, 'Peter took him and began to *rebuke* him.' *

'A 'reprimand' is always addressed to inferiors, and has a stronger sense than either of the former words. It is understood to imply something of an *official* reproof, and from one having authority.

'Censure' has less of *personality* than any of these words; it is rather the expression of an unfavorable opinion

---

* The nouns and verbs are here used indifferently, as they precisely correspond.

than a direct 'reproof.' The conduct of a public man is 'censured' in the papers; an author is 'censured in a review. It always applied to the opinion of equals, or to those who judge *as* equals, even if they are not really so. We never 'censure' an inferior, and in 'censuring' a superior, we place ourselves for the time on an equality with him.

'Remonstrance' and 'expostulation' are both more argumentative, and have more of the character of advice than any of the other words mentioned. They have also this characteristic, that they always imply an attempt to dissuade their object from some action or line of conduct which is either taking place, or about to take place, — some step which a person is about to take; while 'censure' applies to what is *past*. We might say, 'his conduct deserves *censure*, for he acted as he did in spite of the *remonstrances* (or *expostulations*) of his friends.'

The chief difference between these two words is, that a 'remonstrance' may be used with a superior, while 'expostulation' is more generally applied to an equal or inferior.

A 'reproach' differs from all the other words mentioned in three ways. First, it is more personal. A 'reproof' is always supposed to be given for the benefit of the person reproved; a 'reproach' is often merely a vent to the feelings of the person who gives it. Secondly, it is not limited to any grade or relation, but may be given to equals, superiors, or inferiors. A child may reproach a parent with his neglected education; a king may reproach his subjects for their desertion — his allies for their faithlessness. Thirdly, 'reproach' differs in respect of its object. To reproach a person, is to attribute a fault to him which *he does not admit;* while to reprove him is to dwell on the wrong he has done in committing it. Thus, we *reprove* the Romanists for their idolatry; we *reproach* some professed members of our own Church with being Romanists at heart.

ANSWER, REPLY, REJOINDER.

An 'answer' and a 'reply' *may* be synonymous, but are not always so. In general, we are said to 'answer' a *question*, and to 'reply' to an *attack*. The first time a question is responded to, it is always called an 'answer;' but if this, again, is 'answered,' the 'answer' to the 'answer' is called a 'reply.' A 'rejoinder' is an 'answer' given in support of some former 'answer.' It is chiefly used as a law-term, but in general it implies something said in a later stage of the debate or discussion, rather than a 'reply.' But 'answer' (whether used as a noun or as a verb) is used in a secondary sense, to imply something which serves the purpose for which it was said — which satisfies the questioner, confutes or silences the objector, defeats the opponent, &c.

A 'reply' is merely something said in return, or by way of an 'answer' to some question, attack, &c. Hence we say, 'this *reply* is *no answer;*' 'Many books have been written in *reply* to this author, but he has never yet been *answered*.'

A COMMAND, INJUNCTION, ORDER.

'Command' is the most general term of the three. We speak of a 'divine command,' rather than 'injunction' or 'order.' 'Injunction' relates more to general conduct; 'order' to particular acts. A child receives 'orders to learn his lesson, but 'injunctions' to be diligent and attentive. We should not speak of giving a servant 'orders,' but 'injunctions' to be tidy. A 'command,' though not more absolute or despotic than an 'order' or 'injunction,' generally indicates persons of a higher station: a king or general issues 'commands;' an inferior officer gives 'orders.'

'Commandment,' the other noun derived from the verb 'to command,' is now nearly obsolete, and used only for the laws laid down in the Bible. The original meaning of our word 'command' seems to have been 'power' or authority. (See SHAKSPEARE, *King Lear.*)

DEFERENCE, RESPECT, VENERATION.

'Deference' may be felt for those whose general character we neither 'respect' nor 'venerate.' It is often entertained unconsciously, and is nothing more than an habitual *presumption in favor* of a person's opinions; a feeling rather than an opinion, that he is more likely to be right than another. We may feel 'deference' for a person on *particular points* only; for instance, we should defer to, or feel deference for, a sailor in matters connected with the sea, or a lawyer in questions of law. But 'respect' and 'veneration' must be felt for the *whole character* of their object. These two last words approach each other in their meaning; but 'veneration' is a much stronger sentiment than 'respect.' We may both 'respect' and 'venerate' those for whom we have no 'deference;' but this is a circumstance rarely if ever acknowledged, even to ourselves.*

Lastly, 'respect' and 'veneration' are felt exclusively for *moral* qualities, to which 'deference' is not confined. We should not think of respecting such a man for his mathematical talents, or venerating another for his skill in some work of art; but in both these cases we might feel 'deference.'

Conjugate words. — The conjugates 'respectable' and 'venerable' have considerably diverged from the meaning of their roots. 'Respectable' is almost the lowest term of approbation we can use; and 'venerable' is always applied

---

* See Whately's *Rhetoric,* under the head 'Deference.'

to something ancient; whereas, we may 'venerate' virtue, whether in youth or age. 'Deferential' is merely applied to *manners*. The verbs strictly correspond with the nouns.

ILLUSION, DELUSION.

'Illusion' has most to do with visions of the imagination: 'delusion' with some decided mental deception. An 'illusion' is an idea which is presented before our bodily or mental vision, and which does not exist in reality. A 'delusion' is a false view entertained of something which really exists, but which does not possess the quality or attribute erroneously ascribed to it.

'Delusions' may likewise be applied to perverted *opinions*. A fanatic sectarian is said to be possessed by 'delusions.' 'Illusions,' on the other hand, are solely applied to the visions of a distempered imagination, the chimerical ideas of one blinded by hope, passion, or credulity — or, lastly, to spectral and other occular deceptions, to which the word 'delusion' is never applied.

FALSEHOOD, FALSITY.

'Falsity' is, properly speaking, the *quality* of a false proposition; 'falsehood,' the proposition itself. When we have found out that a person has told a 'falsehood,' we are convinced of the 'falsity' of his assertion. The educated classes are very apt to use the word 'falsehood' for 'falsity;' as 'I perceive the *falsehood* of your declaration.' The vulgar fall into the reverse error, and sometimes speak of 'telling a *falsity*.'

DECEIT, DECEPTION, FRAUD.

'Deception' is used for *individual instances*, or *acts*, of one who deceives; 'deceit,' for the acts, and also from the habit of mind, or for the act when continued and repeated.

We speak of 'a long course of *deceit*,' but of 'an *act* of *deception*.' 'Deception' is likewise used more in respect of the effect produced on the *person deceived;* 'deceit' with regard to the agent, or deceiver. 'Deception' may therefore be used in cases where no guilt is implied; we speak of a 'deception' of the senses, an optical 'deception, &c.* 'Deceit' could not be used in these instances, as it always has a reference to the *intention* of the agent. The conjugate 'deceptive' is generally applied to illusions of the senses.

'Fraud' is always used for an individual *act* of deceit: 'a system of fraud' is a series of such individual acts.

ADMITTANCE, ADMISSION.

'Admittance' is almost invariably applied to a literal permission to enter some place, and is never used figuratively. 'Admission' is more general in its signification, and is used both in a literal and in a figurative sense; as, 'to make some *admissions* on a disputed subject.' But even in the literal sense, in which either 'admittance' or 'admission' may be used, they somewhat differ in their shades of meaning.

'Admittance' is, in fact, a *right* to 'admission.' When a ticket of 'admittance' to some show or sight is given, it implies merely a permission to enter: when we *have* entered, we have obtained 'admission;' 'admittance' was gained as soon as the ticket was ours.

COMPULSION, COERCION, RESTRAINT, CONSTRAINT.

'Compulsion' and 'coercion' are more active in their signification than the two other terms mentioned; that is to say, they imply a positive as well as negative force. We

* See the article on the adjectives, DECEITFUL, &c.

are 'restrained' *from* doing something we should wish to do; but we are 'coerced,' or 'compelled,' to act in some way against our will. A prisoner is *compelled* to work in a house of correction; he is *restrained* from escaping.*

Secondly, 'compulsion' and 'coercion' are never used to express the force a person exercises on *himself*, but only in relation to others; 'restraint' and 'constraint' may be applied to ourselves.

There is a difference again, between 'compulsion' and 'coercion.' 'Compulsion' is actual force, used directly to induce others to act as we would have them do; 'coercion' is a more remotely exercised force, being an appeal to the passion of fear, &c. A government is said to use 'coercion' to make its subjects profess the established form of religion; a traveller in the hands of robbers gives up his purse, or signs an order for a ransom, under 'compulsion.' It is true that, in both cases, the object may be gained by awakening the same kind of fear: but the word 'coercion' directs the attention rather to the moral or mental, and 'compulsion' to the physical force employed.

'Constraint' differs from 'restraint,' chiefly in implying a resistance of the *will* to the force used. 'Restraint,' when applied to the power we exercise on *ourselves*, generally implies that force which is exerted by an inward principle of self-control; while 'constraint,' though it may be exercised on ourselves, proceeds from some *external* cause, supplying the motive. A man of frail temper 'restrains' himself to a sense of duty; but he is 'constrained; to control himself by the presence of those whom he fears, respects, or regards with suspicion. We exercise 'constraint' on ourselves *unwillingly*: a 'constrained' manner always implies a manner acted upon by some influence from without,

* The verbs here correspond with the nouns.

not by any inward motive — a curb put on the manner. It is therefore generally applied to *outward* indications; whereas 'restraint' may be exercised on the feelings or passions.

'Constraint' is always personal; 'restraint' may be applied to the emotions or feelings. A man is *himself* 'constrained;' we should not say that his *feelings* were 'constrained;' his feelings, or emotions, are 'restrained.'

Again, 'constraint' is positive, 'restraint' negative; hence the passage in the Bible, 'The love of Christ *constraineth* us.' * We could not say, 'restraineth' us, unless it were *from* doing anything to which we were tempted. A person is 'restrained' *from* some action, and 'constrained' *to* do it.

DETERMINATION, RESOLUTION, DECISION.

'Decision' differs from the other two words in implying a choice between several courses of action, which the others do not.

We 'decide' † between opposite courses, we 'determine' what to do, and 'resolve' to carry out our 'determination.' 'Determination' is a lower kind of 'decision.' 'Resolution' has more of a moral character. A 'resolution' taken is a promise made to oneself. A stubborn man is 'determined.' A firm man is 'resolved.' A man who is quick in forming a judgment, and firm in adhering to it, is 'decided.' A 'resolute' or a 'decided' character both imply something higher than a 'determined' one.

These three substantives have in fact two meanings; one implying the *act* of 'resolving,' or 'deciding,' or 'determin-

---

* In old English, the verb 'constrain' was used in a wider sense than it is now, being often used where we should now use the words 'urge' or 'persuade.'

† The conjugate verbs and adjectives have corresponding senses with the substantives.

ing,' the other, the *habit.* We have been considering the latter, which would, however, be better expressed by 'resoluteness,' 'decisiveness,' &c.

NARRATION, NARRATIVE, RELATION, ACCOUNT, HISTORY, TALE.

'Narrative' and 'narration' are nearly the same, and are the widest in their meaning of all the group. 'Relation' is also nearly synonymous with them, but is less frequently used, being more French than English. An 'account' is always a report of some individual event, and is only used when its connexion with the event alluded to is decidedly expressed. We may speak generally of an interesting 'narrative' or 'narration,' but an account must always be *of* some incident, its connexion with which is never lost sight of or left to be understood.

A 'record' is a report of some event, or series of events, made for the purpose of reference,—something of the nature of a memorandum of a fuller kind.

A 'history' must always be a connected account of a series of events, generally one of some length. The incidents recorded in it must be of some importance in themselves—we should not speak of the 'history' of any trivial occurrence, except ironically. The expression 'family history' is no exception to this rule, for it *has* a relative importance, though only of a private character; but 'history' is more usually and correctly appropriated to public events. It is always used for a general outline, whereas 'account' must be particular. We should say, 'in the *history* of this author we have an *account* of such and such a battle.'

The events related in history are always at least *supposed* to be true; whereas the word 'story' is generally (though not universally), applied to evident and apparent fiction, or to something, at all events, of *doubtful* truth. For instance, we say, 'I will tell you the *history* of my life;' but 'he told me a *long story* of what had happened to him, which I did not believe.'

The three words, 'history,' 'story,' and 'narrative,' are however often used synonymously.

'Tale' is nearly the same as 'story,' but implies fiction still more decidedly and *necessarily*. We always speak of a 'fairy-tale,' 'a legendary tale,'—'story' in this case would not be used. The expression, 'he told me the whole *story*,' would not necessarily imply fiction; if the word 'tale' were substituted, it certainly would, The only exception, indeed, to this word's implying fiction, is the expression, 'tale-bearing,' or 'tale-telling.'

DISPLAY, SHOW, PARADE, OSTENTATION.

'Display' is the only one of these four terms which does not necessarily imply *excess;* for though the expression 'a love of display' is sometimes used in that sense, yet we frequently speak of 'a display' of talent or beauty, without meaning to convey the idea of blame by the term. 'Display, is not limited to any one class of subjects, but is equally used in material and in abstract cases. 'This man is clever, but is too fond of the *display* of his talents;' 'the song she sang was well fitted for the *display* of her powers of voice:' 'the peacock seems to delight in the *display* of his fine plumage.'

'Show,' when used *by itself*, is always applied to an appearance of outward and material splendor—either something that indicates wealth, or an *imitation* of it;* we say, for instance, 'wealth is too often wasted in idle *show*—a love of *show* and brilliancy has ruined many.'

---

* The adjective 'showy' corresponds with this sense of the word 'show.'

'Show,' however, when used in conjunction with another substantive, is more like 'display' in its meaning, but conveys also the idea of fiction. A 'show' of piety must be feigned. One who really gives munificently may make a 'display' of his liberality; but if he were said to 'make a *show* of liberality,' it would imply that he only *appeared* to give, while he really kept back his money.

'Parade' may be applied either to material objects or to mental qualifications; in both cases it indicates an excessive and absurd display and boasting — which forces the things 'displayed' upon the public notice in an offensive manner. A refined person may be fond of 'show,' or inclined to 'display:' 'parade' is always vulgar. 'Ostentation,' which was the same in its original sense as 'show,' now generally indicates a parade of virtues or other qualities for which we expect to be honored. The conjugate adjective, 'ostentatious,' is more commonly applied to outward and material splendor, and the substantive to a display of virtue; but either may be used for either.

IMAGINATION, CONCEPTION, FANCY.

'Imagination' and 'fancy' are frequently confounded together, but are, nevertheless, very distinct in their signification. In the first place, 'imagination' implies more of a *creative* power than 'fancy;' it requires a greater combination of various powers, and is therefore a higher exercise of genius. 'Fancy,' on the other hand, is more an employment of ingenuity and taste, though it also requires inventive power. Secondly, 'imagination' implies a longer flight; 'fancy,' rather a succession of short efforts: the one is a steady blaze, the other a series of sparkles. An epic poem would require an exercise of the first; a ballad, or other lighter production, of the last. Hence we may see that, as it has been well remarked,* the difference between the two is, in some measure, one of subject-matter; for the same power which we call 'fancy,' when employed in a melody of Moore, would be called 'imagination' in the works of Dante or Milton.

In short, the efforts of 'fancy' bear the same relation to those of 'imagination' that the carving and polishing of a gem or seal does to sculpture.

In the third place, *wit* may come into works of 'fancy,' and could not be admitted into the province of 'imagination.' The same with what are called *conceits.*

'Conception' has something in common with imagination, but it implies more decidedly a creative power, and is referred to something tangible and real; whereas, in efforts of fancy and imagination, there is always a consciousness of unreality. The province of 'conception' is that which has a real existence. Hence, the productions of painters, sculptors, and musicians are called 'conceptions.'

'Conception' also denotes something framed and originated in our *own* mind; whereas the imagination or fancy may be acted on merely from without. The poet or writer of fiction exercises his own conceptions, but awakens the imagination of his readers.

CONVICTION, PERSUASION.

'Conviction' is the act of the *understanding;* 'persuasion' of the *will.* 'Conviction' is effected by such a train of argument as will bring the understanding to admit the conclusion to which it leads; 'persuasion' is effected by exhortation, whose office it is to enlist the feelings and *will* in the orator's service. The first is the province of logic,

---

* See an interesting article in the *Edinburgh Review* for April, 1842, on Moore's *Poems.*

the second of rhetoric; but it is a mistake to suppose, as many do, that they can be exercised independently of each other, in reference *to action.*

To induce men to act as we would have them do, two conditions are requisite: first, they must be shown that certain means are essential, or at least the best possible, towards a certain end; and, secondly, that the end to be attained *is* desirable.* It would be no use to prove to an army that such and such means were likely to enable them to conquer the enemy, unless they were inspired with the *desire* of victory; and, on the other hand, the most animating exhortations to bravery and daring would not induce them to a certain mode of procedure, unless they thought it conducive to that object.

But often one-half of the desired effect has been already accomplished, and we have only the other half to perform: the auditors are already convinced, and we have only to exhort, — or, their feelings or desires sufficiently excited, and we have only to convince them of the best means for accomplishing the end in view.

Hence, it is a mistake to say that the wisest of mankind are governed by reason, and the majority by their feelings; for the wise could not act on their convictions, unless their *will* were influenced; and the multitude are *convinced* as well as impelled by feeling, though they are often led by their passions to accept bad and inconclusive reasoning as convincing.

The real state of the case is, that the wisest and best of mankind use their reason to bring their will and feelings under control, while the unthinking crowd allow their feelings to take captive their reason, and are first excited, and then convinced on insufficient grounds.

---

* See Whately's *Rhetoric,* Part II., chap. i, § 1.

'Persuasion,' then, is the wider term of the two: it *includes* both 'conviction,' and that excitement of feeling which leads to *action;* while 'conviction' *alone* is inactive. Formerly, 'persuasion' was used much as 'conviction' is now, as we may see in some passages of our Bible translation. From the old use of the word probably arose the expression, 'religious *persuasion;*' though it might almost pass for a satire on the proneness of mankind to follow their feelings rather than their reason in matters of religious belief.

GOODNESS, VIRTUE.

These words are used indiscriminately; but when their meaning is distinct, 'goodness' is usually applied to that which is natural and without effort, and 'virtue' to the merit which springs from self-discipline, and a steady resistance to temptations which are felt to be strong.*

One who had been brought up as a thief would be doing a *virtuous* action in abstaining from depredation; if, by long-continued efforts, his character at last so improved that theft was odious instead of tempting to him, he would perform fewer virtuous acts, but his 'goodness' would be greater. '*Goodness of heart*' is, indeed, used to express a mere passive benevolence; but 'goodness,' in the *abstract*, is used to express a higher excellence than 'virtue.' We can venture to apply the term to the Supreme Being; whereas 'virtue' is purely a *human* quality. As long as we live on

---

* A very pleasing description of untutored natural *goodness* of disposition may be found in Wordsworth's *Ode to Duty:*

> 'Glad hearts, without reproach or blot,
> Who do thy will and know it not.'

The word 'virtue' could not be applied to this instinctive kind of goodness: nor could it be applied to the *highest* kind; it seems to indicate a middle state.

this earth, the best must spend their lives in resisting and struggling against temptations, and controlling evil tendencies; but in sinless perfection there can be no *virtue*.

HINDRANCE, OBSTACLE, IMPEDIMENT.

A 'hindrance' holds us back when we are about to start forward: an 'obstacle' is found in our path, and opposes us when we *have* started: an 'impediment' makes our further progress more difficult, and *hampers* us in what we wish to do; whence the Romans called their baggage *impedimenta*. A weight carried is an 'impediment;' a bar thrown across the road is an 'obstacle:' an importunate visitor who prevents our setting out is a 'hindrance.' We might say, 'I had so many *hindrances* before starting that I could not set out as early as I wished; I had many things to carry with me, and this was an *impediment* to my speed; the *obstacles* I met with on the road tempted me to turn back.'

A 'hindrance' or 'impediment' may be merely of a *material* kind: an 'obstacle' is something decidedly hostile, and set in opposition to us. Even when the 'obstacle' is inanimate, we, as it were, personify it for the time, and consider it in the light of something intentionally hostile. Hence, the expressions we use in connexion with these words are different. We *remove* an 'impediment' or 'hindrance;' we *surmount* an 'obstacle.' We proceed *notwithstanding* an 'impediment' or hindrance;' *in spite of* an 'obstacle.'

ALLEGIANCE, LOYALTY.

'Allegiance' is a principle of action; 'loyalty' a sentiment. 'Loyalty' is also more personal, and is more limited to our relation to a hereditary monarch: 'allegiance' would apply equally to any form of government, merely implying fidelity and obedience. In short, 'loyalty' is a faithful adherence to some individual monarch or ruler *as such;* 'allegiance,' fidelity to any government, old or new, monarchical or republican, to which we have *sworn* obedience. The words are originally the same,* indicating obedience to law, and thereby showing how little the light thrown by derivations on the modern meaning of a word can be trusted.

SECURITY, SAFETY, SURETY.

'Security' has preserved something of its etymological meaning (*securus*, without care); it implies an absence of all fear or anxiety, but not necessarily absence of danger; for there may be a *false* security.

By 'safety' we understand a well-grounded security; an absence of *danger*, not merely of the *sense* of danger. We might say, 'They believed themselves in a place of *safety*, but theirs was a false *security*.'

'Security' has, however, another sense, which is nearly synonymous with 'surety;' both referring to precautions taken to *ensure safety*. The adjective 'secure,' and the verb 'to secure,' are not conjugate with the noun 'security,' but rather with 'safety.'

The adjective 'sure' is a contraction of 'secure,' and when applied to things and places is synonymous with it; when to persons, it implies a strong *conviction*, but not certain knowledge.

REFORMATION, REFORM.

'Reformation' is generally applied to great occasions; to the amendment of principles, articles of belief, or points affecting the highest and gravest interests of a nation or in-

* Some consider 'allegiance' to be derived from *alligo,* to bind: this derivation, however, is by others considered doubtful.

dividual. 'Reform' is oftener applied to practical details. We speak of a 'reformation' in religion, but of a 'reform' in government; of the 'reformation' of a criminal, but of a 'reform' in the management of a household, or administration of business. A man whose *character* has undergone a complete 'reformation,' will generally effect a 'reform' in his habits and way of life.

It is a recent custom to speak of 'reforming' abuses; but this is an impropriety of language; abuses may be remedied, or extirpated, but they cannot be 'reformed.' In the same way, we speak improperly of '*curing* diseases;' it is, correctly speaking, the *patient* who is cured.

FAITH, BELIEF, CERTAINTY.

'Belief' is merely an assent of the understanding, in which the *will* is not concerned: and this is the chief distinction between it and faith.

Faith may, however, be said to have, besides this, three distinguishing characteristics.

First, — It must be a belief founded on *authority:* this does not imply a blind assent, in the absence of proof: for we may have good and sufficient evidence for the trustworthiness of our authority. It is often supposed that faith, to be perfect, requires that reason should be put aside or kept in subjection: but this would be to make *credulity* a a necessary accompaniment of faith. It is too often found so combined: but the highest faith is not of this nature. The true test of its merit and virtue is, not assenting to anything against our *reason*, but against our *prejudices* or *interests.*

Secondly, — Faith implies an assent to a system or series of propositions, not to one insulated fact. Our trust in the assertion of some one who was administering medicine to us, that he had taken a certain bottle from a certain shelf, would not be called *faith ;* though our reliance on his general mode of practice would be so designated.*

Thirdly, — Faith is generally of a *practical* nature. We do not speak of having 'faith' in the Copernican system, though we may believe it firmly on authority, because it does not directly lead to any course of action: but one who had been induced by the representations of its earliest followers to attempt a voyage round the world, would be justly said to have 'faith' in what they told him, because he not only held their opinions in theory, but followed them up in practice.

Hence a mere assent to the truths of Christianity, such as we give to any mere historical fact, and which does not affect the conduct, cannot be called 'faith.'

'Certainty' is generally applied to a firm conviction of the truth of any proposition: but when opposed to 'belief' or 'faith,' it describes more correctly that conviction which is only produced by demonstration, or the evidence of the senses.

'Certainty' has come to be applied by a metonymy to the *thing*, which is the *object* of a certain belief.

FORGIVENESS, PARDON.

As is usually the case where a Saxon and a Latin word are used in nearly the same sense, the Saxon word gives the more forcible, homely, and serious meaning — the Latin, on the other hand, the more polite and colloquial one.

Both 'forgiveness' and 'pardon' are alike used, it is true, in a religious sense; but in ordinary life 'pardon' is applied in more trifling matters than 'forgiveness.' We beg a person's 'pardon' for jostling him in a crowd: we ask his 'forgiveness' for having seriously injured him.

---

* The primary notion of faith would seem to be, trust in a *person.*

It is remarkable that the words in all European languages which express 'forgiveness' or 'pardon,' all imply *free gift.*

FEELINGS, SENTIMENTS.

'Sentiments' are used in a wider sense than 'feelings,' including not only what are strictly called 'matters of *feeling*,' but also matters of opinion of one kind; viz., those in which feelings are concerned. Thus, we speak of our sentiments on religious, political, or moral questions; but we should not speak of 'sentiments' on chemistry or mathematics. 'Sentiments' are never spoken of alone and in the abstract, except in reference to the *natural* moral faculties, in a physiological sense. We speak of a person as having 'strong' or 'lively' *feelings*, but never as having strong 'sentiments.'

SPEECH, ORATION, HARANGUE, DISCOURSE.

A member of Parliament makes a 'speech;' a king is received by a deputation, whose leader makes an 'oration' in his honor; a popular leader makes an 'harangue' to a mob. A 'speech' is the simplest mode of delivering one's sentiments; an 'oration' is an elaborate and prepared speech; an 'harangue' is a vehement appeal to the passions of the persons addressed, or a speech which has something disputatious and combative in it.

A 'discourse' is a set speech on some subject which is intended to convey instruction to the listeners. It differs from the other three in being applied to what is written — the others are only spoken.

PITY, COMPASSION, SYMPATHY.

'Pity' and 'compassion' resemble each other very nearly in their signification; but there is a shade of difference. 'Pity' often implies an approach to contempt; 'compassion' has more of tenderness in it. We may speak of *pitying* the wicked, or the hopelessly foolish; we only speak of *compassionating* those into whose feelings we can enter, and whose actions we may conceive ourselves performing. Again, 'compassion' is sometimes felt for imaginary sorrows; 'pity' seldomer.

'Sympathy' implies more of fellow-feeling than either of the other terms, and is not restricted to subjects of pain, but may be equally felt for the pleasures of others.

A certain degree of equality in station, age, mind, or qualities, is essential. We cannot feel *sympathy* with any but one who is nearly an equal; we may feel *compassion* for a superior or inferior likewise; we *pity*, generally, only one whom we regard as in some way an inferior.* Great admiration and pity cannot be felt at the same time for the same person. No one could pity a martyr, or a hero nobly dying for his country. The proper object of 'pity,' as has been well observed by an eminent writer,† is suffering not *wholly* unmerited, but occasioned rather by weaknesses than faults; its most fitting subject is a character of mixed good and evil, being neither of a very high nor low order — like Shakspeare's *Lear*, for example, or Scott's *Amy Robsart.*

MODESTY, DIFFIDENCE, HUMILITY.

'Modesty' and 'humility' are virtues; 'diffidence' is not in itself a virtue; and, in some cases, even amounts to a defect. It implies a great, sometimes even an excessive,

* Hence, a high-spirited person feels it a degradation to be the object of *pity*. Scott has alluded to this feeling in the *Lady of the Lake*, —

> 'And last, and worst to spirit proud,
> Had borne *the pity of the crowd*.'

† In one of the numbers of the *Quarterly Review*. The doctrine is Aristotle's, to whom the reviewer refers.

distrust of our own powers. A diffident man will shrink from doing that which he is perfectly equal to perform, from an unreasonable dread of failure. 'Modesty' does not imply self-distrust, but simply an unwillingness to put ourselves forward, and an absence of all over-confidence in our own powers. A modest man may feel a proper confidence in his own powers, but he will not be eager to display them. He will rather shrink from notice than court it, and when called to any post of distinction, he will 'bear his honors meekly,' and make no attempt to claim even the deference which might fairly be due to him.

And here it may be remarked, thnt the jealousy felt by the generality of mankind towards superior talents is such, that a man of eminent abilities is scarcely forgiven for rating himself as he deserves — though one of moderate intellect is allowed to do so.

'Humility' somewhat resembles 'modesty,' but it implies rather a *readiness* to *yield our claims*, than a *reluctance* to court notice. 'Humility' is often falsely defined to be a disposition to underrate ourselves; but this is a mistake. There is no *humility* in a clever man's thinking himself a fool; in fact, such a mistaken estimate is more likely to lead to a restless, irritable vanity. Real humility consists in rating our own *claims* low — in being willing to waive our rights, and descend to a lower place than might be our due; in being ready to admit our liability to error, and listening patiently to objections, even when they thwart our views; in freely owning our faults when conscious of having been wrong, and, in short, in not being over-careful of our own dignity.

Finally, we may consider that the opposite to 'diffidence' is confidence; the opposite to 'modesty,' impudence or assurance; the opposite to 'humility,' pride or conceit.

AUSTERITY, SEVERITY, RIGOR, STERNNESS, STRICTNESS.

'Austerity' and 'strictness' are the only ones among these terms which apply to the mode of life. 'Strictness' is 'rigor,' in the sense of a particular adherence to rules, and steadiness in enforcing them. It also usually implies a disposition to multiply rules and prohibitions, — to restrict liberty. 'Austerity' is chiefly used in reference to the person characterized. 'Severity' is almost exclusively applied to our judgments of, or conduct to, others. 'Rigor' may either mean an excess of severity, or great strictness in adhering to rules.

A hermit leads a life of *austerity;* a parent or teacher may treat his children or pupils with *severity;* the laws under a despotic government are enforced with *rigor.* 'Rigor' does not necessarily imply severity, but only strictness; a government may enforce moderate rules with rigor.

The opposite to 'rigor' is 'relaxation,' as 'lax' is to 'rigorous;' the opposite of 'severity' is 'mildness;' that of 'austerity' — as relating to our conduct with others — is 'indulgence;' but *personal* austerity has no opposite, except that which points out a blameable excess on the one side, as self-indulgence, or luxuriousness. The medium, in which, as Aristotle says, virtue lies, is nameless.*

'Sternness' is more applicable to character and manners than to judgment and actions. A man of stern disposition shows it to all with whom he comes in contact, whether offenders or not.

---

* It may, perhaps, be suggested, that the word 'temperance' would express this medium; but the use of this word by itself is almost entirely confined to moderation in eating and drinking; and it would, therefore, be more appropriately described as a medium between 'intemperance' and 'abstemiousness,' than between 'austerity' and 'self-indulgence,' which apply to every part of a person's life, and are not restricted to the gratification of the appetite.

The two following groups of synonyms (with the exception of the paragraph on 'cleverness') are quoted from the *Diary of Sir James Mackintosh*, whose definitions cannot be improved upon: —

'GENIUS, WISDOM, ABILITIES, TALENTS, PARTS, INGENUITY, CAPACITY,' CLEVERNESS.

'*Genius* is the power of new combination, and may be shown in a campaign, a plan of policy, a steam-engine, a system of philosophy, or an epic poem. It seems to require seriousness, and some dignity in the purpose; on ludicrous subjects it is called wit; and in weaving together the parts of an argument, or the incidents of a tale, it receives the inferior name of *ingenuity*.

'*Wisdom* is the habitual employment of a patient and comprehensive understanding in combining various and remote means to promote the happiness of mankind. It is most properly applied to him who actually renders signal services of the most difficult nature to society. It is well used to denote the teachers of moral and political truth, because the inculcation of such truth must in process of time produce its practical application. It is also applied to those who improved the general modes of exerting intellect, from a just, though not perhaps distinct, perception of the ultimate tendency of intellectual cultivation to increase the means of happiness, and to improve the moral nature of man. But to mere speculation, or to those sciences of which the professors have no immediate reference to human improvement, this high and august term cannot be applied. It is the loftiest and most venerable of all terms of commendation, because it is the only word for intellectual superiority, which necessarily includes a moral tendency, if not a virtuous purpose. It is the highest exertion of reason for the most pure end.

'*Abilities* may be exerted in conduct, or in the arts and sciences, but rather in the former; and when the term is applied to the latter, it is rather in the practical sense of attaining a particular object, that in that of general excellence.

'*Talents* are the power of executing well a conception, either original or adopted. They may be possessed in a degree very disproportioned to general power, as habit may strengthen a mind for one sort of exertion far above its general vigor.

'*Parts* have lost a considerable portion of their dignity. They were used in the last century perhaps almost in the sense in which we now rather employ talents. They at present, if at all used, might signify a specious sort of smartness.

'*Capacity* is a power of acquiring. It is most remarkable in the different degrees of facility with which different men acquire a language.

'Sir Isaac Newton and Milton are equally men of genius. Bacon is the wisest of writers, not only because he is so great a teacher of moral and civil wisdom, but because he has contributed more than any other man to the general improvement of the human understanding. Sir Isaac Newton had the highest philosophical genius, but the sciences on which he employed it do not allow the praise of wisdom. Sir Robert Walpole and Lord Godolphin were ministers of great abilities, though they did not possess either the brilliant talents of Bolingbroke, or the commanding genius of Chatham.'

'Cleverness' (derived evidently from the verb to *cleave**)

---

* It is curious to observe, that several of the words which describe the various mental powers are derived from words signifying to split, cleave, or separate; as science from *scio,* probably the same as *scindo,* to cut: clever, from *cleave:* distinguish, discriminate, both signifying a dividing or sifting process, &c.

is correctly applied to a certain quickness and readiness in the operations of the mind, and especially in the act of acquiring knowledge. But the loose way in which ideas are expressed in ordinary conversation has led to a considerable abuse of this word, which is not seldom applied to every kind of talent.

'FORTITUDE, COURAGE, VALOR, BRAVERY, INTREPIDITY, GALLANTRY, HEROISM.

'*Fortitude* is the most comprehensive of these words. It is always used morally, and is the name of a virtue which consists in the babit of bearing pain and encountering danger. It is often confined to the endurance of pain, and is used almost synonymously with patience, though it rather indicates a spirit that resists pain, than one which submits to it. *Courage* is active *fortitude*, and is shown against every sort of danger. *Bravery* and *valor* are both *courage*, exhibited against the danger of death from a living opponent; *bravery*, perhaps, extends to all living opponents; *valor* is certainly confined to human adversaries, and chiefly, if not solely, in regular war. Firm *courage* is *intrepidity;* adventurous *courage* is *gallantry*. The contempt of danger, not from ignorance or inconsiderate levity, but from just confidence in the power of overcoming the peril, is *heroism*. *Fortitude* is one of those moral qualities, which, on account of their eminent importance, were called by the ancients cardinal virtues. Regulus showed a determined *fortitude* when he returned to death rather than violate his pledged word.

'*Courage* may be shown by a seaman who braves the dangers of the sea, or by a horseman who mounts a horse which no one else will approach.

'*Valor* and *bravery* can only be displayed against *present* danger from a *living*—if not a human—adversary. The tortures of Regulus were distant, though certain; he would rather be said to have encountered them with *fortitude.* He might be praised for *courage*, but he would not be called *brave* or *valiant.* He who climbs up a house almost destroyed by fire to save a life may show the greatest *courage*, but not *bravery* or *valor.* It is more natural to say that a man encounters a tiger with *courage*, but perhaps there is no impropriety in saying that he showed *bravery.* *Bravery* may be proved in single combat; *valor* is the *courage* of a soldier in war — it cannot be applied to single combats. A defence is 'intrepid,' and seems scarcely to be 'gallant,' unless we consider the attacks by which the defence is carried on; it is in attack that *gallantry* is shown.

'The consciousness of power which forms a hero usually inspires sentiments so elevated, that the word denotes magnanimity and generosity, however irregular, as well as *courage.* We say, indeed, *a barbarous hero*, but it is a phrase which is striking, from the perception of some degree of repugnancy between the parts which compose it.'

LAW, STATUTE, RULE, REGULATION.

A 'law' is a 'rule' formed by the government of a country. A nation is governed by laws; a household by rules. A 'statute' is a 'law' which is solemnly and formally enacted, and distinctly set forth in words. The expression 'statute-law' is opposed to 'common-law,' or law established by long custom. The by-laws of an university are also called 'statutes.'

A 'regulation' is nearly the same as a 'rule,' in its ordinary sense. The enactments of a subordinate body are called 'regulations,' or 'by-laws:' those of a church, 'ordinances.'

'Rule' and 'law' have, however, other meanings besides those we have mentioned, which are sometimes liable to be confounded with them. 'Rule' sometimes implies a governing force or power; as, 'to live under a stern, or a gentle *rule*.' 'Law' is used for an *invariable custom*. It is in this sense we speak of the laws of nature; they are simply certain events which happen invariably, and it is only by observation we can discover them. If one of them was broken through, it would cease to be a law of nature: but a human law is no less a law, however ill it be obeyed.*

CONSOLATION, COMFORT, SOLACE.

'Consolation' and 'comfort' are often synonymous; where they differ, the chief difference between them is, 1st, that 'consolation' has relation chiefly to real afflictions, while 'comfort' may also apply to what mitigates lesser evils, besides including the material and substantial conveniences of life.

2dly, 'Consolation' is used in a more *active* sense than 'comfort.' It implies, generally, the agency of another. We administer 'consolation' to a friend in distress; we exhort him 'to take *comfort*,' not 'to take *consolation*.'

'Solace' differs from both the other words, in being never applied to human agents. We do not 'afford a *solace*' to sufferers, as we may afford consolation, or even comfort. Habits or occupations are most frequently described as affording 'a solace' in trouble; as, for example, 'books are his chief *solace* in his present melancholy situation,'—'the companionship even of a mouse or spider has often been a *solace* to a lonely prisoner.'

GIFT, PRESENT, DONATION.

Where no qualifying clause is inserted, 'gift' is generally understood to imply something of considerable value, and

* See the article 'Law,' in the Appendix to *Elements of Logic*.

'present' something comparatively trifling. A property is conferred by a deed of 'gift;' one friend makes a 'present' to another of some small article of use or ornament.

2dly, a 'present' must be intended as a mark of real or supposed regard, or at least a kind of compliment: a 'gift' may be made without any personal view to its object. An author will sometimes make a 'gift' of some of his works to a library or to a bookseller, merely with a view to circulate them more widely; in such a case the word 'present' would be inappropriate. Any benefit, conferred as it were accidentally, and not of compliment to its object, may be called a 'gift;' hence we speak of 'the *gifts* of nature or of fortune'—not of their 'presents.'

In the common expression, 'a New-year's or Christmas-gift,' 'gift' is used synonymously with 'present.'

A 'donation' is always a 'gift' made to a public charity or other institution.

REASON, CAUSE, SOURCE, ORIGIN.

'Reason' relates, originally, to logical sequence; that which takes place in an argument; as, for instance, 'be always ready to give a *reason* of the hope that is in you.'—(1 Pet. iii. 15.) Strictly speaking, a 'reason' is the cause, not of so and so existing or occurring, but of *our knowing or believing* it: as, the print of a man's footsteps is the 'cause'—not of his having passed that way, but of our knowing it. But in conversation, and sometimes in books, one may find this word employed in the sense of 'cause,' properly so called, viz.: either the physical 'cause,' (that which produces such and such an effect,) or what is called the *final* 'cause,'* (or object aimed at in the production of

* See Whately's *Logic* under the head 'Reason' and 'Cause,' in which this subject is fully discussed.

that effect.) Thus, we may hear people say, 'the *reason* why the days are longest in summer is so and so;' or 'the *reason* why this house was built on high ground was to escape the floods.' But in such expressions, 'cause' would have been more proper. In the latter of these sentences, it is, strictly speaking, the *wish* to avoid floods that caused the choosing of that site for the house.

Though 'reason' is often used for 'cause,' the converse rarely takes place. We seldom find 'cause' put for 'reason.'

'Source' and 'origin' both have reference to physical, not to logical sequence. They are sometimes used indifferently, but in general they preserve the character of their respective etymological derivations. The Latin *surgere*, the root or 'source,' often implies rising, as if from the ground; hence 'source' was used to describe a fountain or spring. And the idea conveyed by a spring, that of *yielding* or *producing* as well as rising, has been preserved in the more abstract meanings of the word. A 'source' of information is not only that from which our information proceeds, but one to which we can *recur*, and from which we can draw fresh stores. If we say, 'the *source* of his strength and resolution is his ardent patriotism,' we imply that the feeling described continually *feeds* the flame it has kindled; but if we said, 'the *origin* of my liking for such a person was so and so,' it might imply that the circumstance from which it had risen, had itself passed away. Hence we speak of the 'origin' not of the 'source,' of a family, a dynasty, a discovery, or a language; but of a 'source of happiness, of information, of interest, or of gain. We might say, 'this or that was the *origin* of the friendship which is now such a *source* of happiness to me.'

Finally 'origin' is perhaps less remote than 'source;'

we call that a 'source' to which something is *ultimately* traced.

SELF-LOVE, SELFISHNESS.

'Self-love' is not only a feeling, but a principle of action; 'selfishness' is a habit. 'Self-love' is a calm, deliberate pursuit of that which is supposed to conduce to our welfare; 'selfishness' is the almost instinctive desire of seeking our own gratification at the moment, without regard to any other consideration. Like all other instincts, it is not far-sighted; as the object of hunger is not happiness, but food, so the object of 'selfishness' is not happiness, but immediate gratification. It will assume different forms, according to the character of its possessor: as has been justly remarked, 'every one has a *self* of his own.' One person will seek glory; another ease; another wealth: the disposition is the same.

'Self-love,' on the other hand, has happiness—as such—for its object, and will sacrifice present pleasure to attain that object; hence, it is implied by a rational nature, and cannot exist without it.

'Selfishness,' however, is applied generally to a disregard of the welfare of others, whether that disregard is shown in grasping at momentary pleasures, or in deliberately following the dictates of 'self-love,' and pursuing our own advantage at the expense of others. In either case, it must be blameable; whereas 'self-love,' if unaccompanied with 'selfishness,' is not necessarily so. Indeed, as Bishop Butler has well remarked,* the world would be better than it is if men had more 'self-love;' it is from the eager pursuit of transient gratifications that most evil takes place, not from the pursuit of happiness, as such.

---

* See Introduction to Butler's *Sermons*.

'Self-love' is sometimes used in another sense, as something compounded of self-esteem and love of approbation — self-respect, heightened by our sense of the estimation in which others hold us. It is in this sense that we speak of 'wounded self-love,' &c.

DISCIPLINE, TRIAL.

These two words have each senses quite remote and unmistakeable; but they have also a sense in which they are occasionally and justly applied to the same things; they then differ in the view taken of the things they qualify.

'Discipline' is given with a view to *training;* as its etymology implies, it is a kind of teaching. A 'trial,' on the other hand, is given to prove the strength or proficiency of its object. A student receives instructions by way of 'discipline;' his examination is a 'trial.' A gun is subjected to various processes to strengthen the metal, which answer to 'discipline;' it is loaded to the muzzle, and fired by way of 'trial,' or proof, as it is called.

But two circumstances cause these two words to be confounded together. One is, that a trial well stood *does* answer the purpose of discipline. A candidate who contends for a prize, or is examined to test his proficiency, is likely to be the better scholar after this trial of skill; and so in other cases.

Secondly, the circumstance of a trial being successfully passed through, is often the cause of *our knowing* the qualifications of the person or thing tried; and we are then apt to think it has been the cause of these qualifications. For example, men and animals in cold, mountainous, and barren districts, are generally strong and hardy; and many imagine that the life of privation they lead actually gives them strength; the fact being, that such a life is not a 'discipline,' but a 'trial.' It is a trial which kills all the weaker ones;

none but the strong can stand it: but as their power of resisting such a life enables us to *see* that they are strong, we are prone to imagine that it *gives* them strength.

The words 'discipline' and 'trial,' are both frequently applied in reference to the crosses and afflictions of life, and not incorrectly, in different senses. Primarily, they may be all said to come under the head of 'trials;' some of them, however, are undoubtedly, in themselves, well calculated for a 'discipline' to the mind. But there are others which have no tendency in *themselves* to make us better, and are rather to be regarded as tests or *trials* of our faith, patience, and Christian principles. Still, if these 'trials' are well borne, they also form a most salutary 'discipline' to us; and we have then reason — from experience, as well as from the teaching of Scripture — to believe that they were intended as such by the wise and merciful Ruler of the world. The word 'discipline' is not, therefore, misapplied in speaking of them; though it should be remembered that they are 'trials' *in themselves*, and 'discipline' only so far as we *make* them such.

ATTACHMENT, AFFECTION, TENDERNESS, FONDNESS, LOVE, LIKING.

'Attachment' is generally used to express a feeling which has more of the character of fidelity than of sentiment: for though often used in precisely the same sense as 'affection,' it is also often used to denote merely a faithful adherence to its object. A man may have a strong 'attachment' to his party, sect, or class: in this sense, the word 'affection' would never be used. A faithful subject would have an 'attachment' to his king — a Highland clansman, to his chief; in all these cases, the word implies devoted fidelity. It is also used in relation to our feeling towards *places*, which is seldom or never the case with 'affection.' And yet, strangely enough, the expression 'an *attachment*,' in the abstract, is frequently used to denote an *affaire de cœur* — the very 'affection' which is generally considered as emphatically more sentimental than constant.

'Affection' is 'attachment,' combined with more warmth and feeling: it is also less restricted in its sense. 'Attachment' is not felt towards inferiors either in age or station: 'affection' may be felt to all. A mother is not said to feel 'attachment,' but 'affection,' for her child.

'Tenderness,' in reference to the words under consideration,* may be considered as a sort of accompaniment to 'affection,' refining that affection by a certain delicacy and softness, and by a thoughtfulness and care, not only for the welfare and real interest of its object, but even for his feelings, his comforts, and smallest pleasures. It can only be shown, in general, by the educated and civilized, because they alone are considerate. A little child, or a barbarian, may be full of 'affection,' but cannot show 'tenderness;' and, in general, the softer and gentler natures possess it most.

'Fondness' originally meant foolishness; and is now generally applied to that caressing kind of affection which has more of demonstration than deep feeling. It is the only one of the words before us, except 'love,' which is used with reference to tastes and pursuits as well as persons; though the adjective 'fond' is oftener used in this sense. But we may have a 'fondness' for gardening or mechanics — for music or painting (though, by the way, this last expression is seldom used by those who are really devoted

* It has two other meanings, one of them nearly conjugate to the adjective 'tender hearted,' which implies an extreme degree of compassion and passive benevolence; the other, implying great carefulness and attention in performing any office.

to the fine arts:) but 'fondness' is never used in reference to higher pursuits, as science or philosophy. It is used in reference chiefly to habits.

'Love' is the most general of all the terms before us; and includes almost all their different meanings; though, in the abstract, usually employed to qualify *one* kind of affection, the being 'in *love*.'

'Love' is also used for a strong desire for the welfare of its object, which may be felt quite apart from any preference of his society or feeling of tenderness. It is in this sense we speak of 'the love of mankind;' in this sense that we are commanded to 'love our neighbour,' 'to love our enemies,' &c. It does not imply any personal knowledge of its object, or any consciousness on the part of that object.

'Liking,' on the other hand, implies a preference for the society of its object quite independent of any wish for his welfare, or any feeling of strong affection. Hence, people are *liked* for very different qualities from those for which they are *loved*. 'Liking' is also extended not only to pursuits and habits, but to inanimate objects, which is not the case with any of the other words under consideration.

REASON, SENSE, UNDERSTANDING.

'Reason' is the most comprehensive of these three words, as it takes in the faculty of 'understanding' in its widest and most abstract signification. But it is used in three senses, which are sometimes overlooked, from their close connexion. The first, as we have said, is that which denotes *all* the intellectual powers collectively; the second, those particular powers which distinguish man from the brutes.* The third, the *arguments* which are *addressed* to the reasoning faculty. This last is the sense in which persons are

* See Appendix to Whately's *Logic*, and *Easy Lessons on Reasoning*.

exhorted to 'hear *reason.*' 'Reason,' in short, in the *second* sense, is the faculty which enables us to understand a 'reason' in the *third* sense.

'Sense' and 'understanding' are used for a certain amount of 'reason.' One who possesses a large share of 'reason' is said to have 'good *sense*,' or a 'good *understanding*.' These two expressions, however, are not synonymous. 'Sense' is both active and passive in its signification; 'understanding,' only passive. 'Understanding' is used for a clear perception of what is *put before us*;* good 'sense' enables us to find out such *things for ourselves.* 'Sense' is accordingly used for judgment in the practical affairs of life; 'understanding' is never so employed. The expression, 'want of *reason*,' implies something different from 'want of *sense*.' One who shows want of 'sense' must be naturally stupid or silly; one who shows want of 'reason' may be so blinded by passion or prejudice as not to make use of the 'sense' he possesses.

GAIETY, LIVELINESS, ANIMATION, VIVACITY.

'Liveliness' and 'gaiety' are, perhaps, the nearest to each other in meaning amongst this group; but there is this great difference between them, that 'gaiety' refers more to a temporary state or mood of mind, 'liveliness' more to the habitual disposition and character. 'Gaiety' is applied by metonymy to those things which are supposed to excite it, such as amusement and dissipation; while 'liveliness' is seldom applied to designate anything but character.

'Animation' appears at first sight to resemble 'liveliness,' but it is, in fact, different. Both *literally* signify 'alive,' but imply it in different senses. An animated person is

---

* See *Proverbs and Precepts*; in which may be found a translation of the lines of Hesiod on the subject.

eager, and easily excited; a lively person is light, gay-spirited, cheerful.

'Vivacity' is something between 'liveliness' and 'animation;' it is less frequently used, being rather recently adopted from the French. In French, it has come to mean something more like 'hot-tempered.'

MISFORTUNE, CALAMITY, DISASTER.

'Misfortune' is the most general of these words, and applies to all kinds of untoward events. 'Calamity' is oftenest applied to some great public or family misfortune, such as famine, or pestilence, or the death or ruin of the head of a household. 'Disaster' is rather more correctly applied to some unfortunate event, occurring as a hindrance to some undertaking or work. A man who loses his property encounters a 'misfortune;' if he meets with losses in some speculation or other enterprise, they are 'disasters;' a war is a great *calamity* to a nation, and entails *misfortunes* on individuals; the defeats and failures incidental to it are 'disasters.'

It is the same with the conjugate words. 'Calamitous' draws the attention to the fact of the *event* itself being unfortunate: 'disastrous' to the evils accompanying it. A war is 'calamitous' in itself: it is 'disastrous' if it turns out ill.

ENVY, EMULATION, JEALOUSY.

All these words relate to sensations of uneasiness produced by the sight of another's advantages, not on *his* account, but on our own. But their exact meaning it is difficult to define, not only because their boundaries, as it were, trench closely on each other, but because the *names* are rendered uncertain by people's proneness to disguise the *thing*. They are unwilling to admit, either to others, or even to themselves, that they are guilty of faults which are so revolting to the ideas of all as 'envy' and 'jealousy,' especially the former.*

'Envy' is a dislike felt towards another, caused by the circumstance of his possessing some good, either not possessed at all by ourselves, or possessed in an inferior degree, or in which the superiority on our side is at least doubtful.

'Emulation,' on the other hand, is a desire to attain, ourselves, an *equal share* of some good which we see another possess, without any dislike to him, or wish to deprive him of it. The actions to which these two feelings give rise are very different: emulation leading us to endeavor to attain a share of the good *for ourselves* which we see another enjoy; envy, to deprive *him* of it. The one has for its object, our own gain; the other, our neighbour's loss. 'Emulation,' accordingly, is not used in reference to every kind of good which can be desired, but only to those things which we may possibly attain by striving. Hence, it is almost limited to honors, power, station, or excellence in any pursuit or moral habit. We are not *emulous* of another's beauty, health, or natural talents, though we may be 'emulous' of his attainments or virtue. But 'envy' may be felt equally for any advantage, whether attainable by ourselves or not.

Many moralists are in the habit of speaking of 'emulation' as a feeling utterly bad in itself; and in support of this opinion the passage from the Epistle to the Galatians is quoted, on '*emulations*, wrath, strife,' &c. But the word in the original, which is here translated 'emulation' (*zelos*)

* This remark has been happily expressed by a German writer: 'No one is envious: envy is something so nasty that no one will touch it. People hate their neighbours from jealousy — from a sense of honor — from a consciousness of dependence — it all comes to the same as envy. But envious! heaven forbid! no one is envious.' — From the *Dramas* of Princess Amalie of Saxony.

is in other parts of the New Testament rendered by 'jealousy,' 'rivalry,' or 'zeal;' and the word is almost as often used in commendation as in blame. Hence, it seems clear that, in the above-mentioned passage, it is used for an unchristian and bitter spirit of rivalry and contention, and not simply for the feeling we understand as 'emulation.' This sentiment is, in moderation, a useful one; it requires, however, to be kept in check, as it is too liable, if indulged to excess, to degenerate into 'envy.'

'Jealousy' is a somewhat ambiguous word, being capable of three different senses, and used both to express a passion and a habit.

First, it is used for a proneness to suspect a slight, or faithlessness, or coldness, in the object of affection — this is the *habit*.

Secondly, for a desire for the exclusive possession of power, influence, approbation, or affection: this is the *passion*.

And thirdly, it is used, though perhaps improperly, for a modification of this passion, in the pain felt by those who feel they have not their just due of affection or preference. A child who sees his parents treat a brother or sister with unjust preference may feel jealous in *this* sense, without having a *jealous temper*. The other two kinds mentioned, — the passion and the habit, — are not necessarily combined, though they are generally found together.

'Jealousy' differs from 'envy' in being *oftener* (though not always) appropriated to cases in which the affections are concerned, and also, in relating more to ourselves and less to others. A person is jealous on his own account, envious on that of another. The person, too, *over* whom (to use an old English expression, which avoids an ambiguity) he is jealous, must always be some one beloved.

There are two or three other sentiments, to express which

we have no very exact words, and which are very apt to be confounded with those we have mentioned, though in reality different, because they all relate to pain felt at another's good fortune.

The first we shall mention is the feeling called by Aristotle *nemesis*. It is an indignation at seeing another possess a good of which he is undeserving, — or of which he makes a bad use, — or which he is incapable of valuing. Those who, like David, 'grieve to see the ungodly in such prosperity,' — or a poor student who sees an ignorant rich man unable to appreciate his splendid library, — alike feel *nemesis*. But, natural and justifiable as is this feeling, it requires, even more than emulation, to be kept in check; for it is the disguise under which envy gains access to the mind; and many will secretly excuse their really *envious* feelings on the ground that they are merely 'indignant' at the sight of ill-bestowed and ill-used advantages. But it is a mistake, not of words, but of things, when this feeling, *in itself*, is called by the name of 'envy.'

Another sentiment of a really blameable kind, which may be considered as in some degree akin to 'envy,' is what may be called 'grudging,' or, to use a polite term, 'exclusiveness,' — the dislike that any one besides ourselves should possess some advantage we value. The lady who is mentioned as having boiled a valuable flower-root before sending it to a friend, to prevent the possibility of her plant being propagated, affords an instance of this disposition; as, also, those persons who suffer a valuable invention to die with them rather than impart it: and the still more numerous class who are in constant dread of any one obtaining possession of a song, a dress, a picture, or an ornament, which they imagine to be their peculiar property. The Greeks included this quality under the name *phthonos*, which also comprised 'envy,' properly so called: *zelos* included 'emulation,' and some kinds of 'jealousy.' The three passions, *phthonos*, *zelos*, and *nemesis*, are discussed and compared together in an admirable portion of Aristotle's *Rhetoric.*

PRIVACY, RETIREMENT, SOLITUDE, SECLUSION, LONELINESS.

'Privacy,' sometimes implies absence from the bustle and state of *public* life; at other times, it is nearly synonymous with 'retirement;' with this difference, that 'privacy' may be occasional and temporary, while 'retirement' always implies some continuance. If we withdraw to our own rooms for an hour, we spend that hour in 'privacy;' 'retirement' refers to the habitual mode of life, and includes not only absence from public life, but even from much general society. One who leads a life of retirement has but few associates, and mixes seldom in the gay world.

'Solitude' and 'seclusion' imply more than this — an entire absence from *all* society; but they imply this in different senses. 'Seclusion' must be, to a certain extent, voluntary;' 'solitude' may be used for a forced absence from society. No one would say that a prisoner alone in his cell, or a shipwrecked man on a desert island, were living in 'seclusion,' but in 'solitude.' 'Seclusion' seems to imply shutting oneself up from the external world, as its derivation indicates (*claudo*, to shut up or close): hence, it is more applicable to a monk, or nun in a convent, than to a hermit in the wilderness. When we say that 'seclusion' is to a certain extent *voluntary*, we do not mean that it is always in accordance with the *wishes* of those who practise it. Many persons submit to a life of seclusion against their inclinations; but still, in such cases no *direct* force is used; they are not compelled, in the sense that a prisoner is compelled, to leave the world.

Correctly speaking, also, 'solitude' is applied to one person alone: 'seclusion' is more properly applied to a small number of persons living together — as a family, or a community, or even the inhabitants of a retired village.

'Loneliness' implies rather the solitude of the heart. We may be *lonely* in a crowd; or, indeed, lonely in a circle of acquaintance — even of connexions, if they are unsympathizing and uninterested in us.

'Privacy' is opposed to publicity.

'Retirement,' to gaiety, or life in the world.

'Solitude,' to the adjective *social*, or to society.

'Seclusion,' to society, in the widest sense.

'Loneliness,' to *sympathetic* companionship.

The adjectives are some of them not strictly conjugate. 'Lonely' applies more to places than persons, though sometimes to the latter. A 'lonely' place is one where we should *feel* lonely. 'Solitary' and 'retired' are also generally applied to places; 'retired' always, except when a person is described as having withdrawn from some public situation — as, a 'retired' officer, or statesman. 'Secluded' is always (correctly speaking) confined to places. 'Private' is *now* more directly opposed to 'public' than is its conjugate noun, 'privacy.' A 'private' interview, letter, or individual, is exactly the opposite to a public one.

EARTH, WORLD, GLOBE.

In speaking of 'the earth,' we refer more to its external and material part: in speaking of 'the world,' to the moral and abstract view of the same thing. In considering the 'earth,' we look at its construction, its natural productions, its geological formation; in comparing our own with other planets or systems, we always speak of 'the earth' — as, 'The *earth* moves round the sun:' in this sense, 'world' would be inadmissible.

The 'world' is rather the 'earth' viewed with reference

to *its inhabitants.* We speak of the providential care and moral government of the 'world,' not of the 'earth:' we might say, 'The wonders and beauties with which the *earth* abounds display the wisdom and goodness of the Creator, but still more his government of the *world.*' And not only is the expression, 'world,' used with reference to mankind in preference to 'earth,' but with reference to man intellectually, in contradistinction to physically. We speak of the various races which inhabit the '*earth*,' but of the 'civilized *world.*' Hence, America was called 'The New *World*,' being viewed with reference to a place that was to be *inhabited.** In speaking of men as forming a community, 'world' is always used instead of 'earth:' as we speak of 'the intellectual, political, theological, or gay world'—or even of 'a poet's *world*'—'the *world* of fancy or of dreams,' &c. Formerly 'earth' was used as 'world' is now, as we may see in our translation of the Psalms, 'The ends of the *earth* shall hear him,' &c.

'Globe' is generally used geologically, and occasionally in poetry.

Lastly, 'earth' is limited to our own planet; but we speak of other 'worlds.' The planets are supposed to be 'worlds;' the starry sky may be full of systems of *worlds;* the abode to which we look for a future life is continually called 'a better *world.*'

This may partly arise from the different derivations of these words. 'Earth' is immediately traceable to the German *erde;* but it is probable that the original root of all was

* There are exceptions to this rule, the principal one being the expression, 'sailing round the world,' which is always used instead of 'earth.' This, probably, arises from the fact, that 'earth' is also generally used synonymously with 'land,' in contradistinction to 'sea,' hence the expression, 'sailing round the earth,' would be somewhat anomalous.

the Hebrew *Erets*, supposed to be derived from a verb signifying to crumble or break in pieces.

'World' (whirled) was evidently expressive merely of *roundness:* as the Latin *mundus* and Greek *cosmos* were of 'order.' *Cosmos* and *mundus* were both used to indicate the *universe.* And it is curious that our derived word, *cosmogony*, always relates to the 'earth,' as distinguished from 'world.' The 'world,' in our modern sense, was rendered in Latin by *seculum*, and in Greek by *aion.*

PROFIT, GAIN, EMOLUMENT.

'Profit' is distinguished from the other two words of this group by being always applied to gain accruing from something that has been laid out first. We speak of 'profits' made by the sale of goods, but not of 'the profits of labor,' or 'winning profits' in a lottery. 'Gain' includes *every* advantage obtained which was not ours before.

'Emolument' is always the reward of labor, and that reward obtained in a regular way, and not by chance.

The history of the derivation of this word is curious: its root is the Latin *mola*, a mill; it was first used to signify anything which could be ground out of a mill; then it came to be figuratively employed, as if to convey the idea of 'grist to the mill,' and so gradually assumed its present sense.

IMPORT, MEANING, SENSE.

The *import* of a speech or book is the idea which it most readily conveys to others; the *meaning* is the idea really intended to be conveyed by the speaker or writer: the *sense* is, either, 1st, The general substance of the whole; or, 2dly, The different ways in which it may be understood, and the ideas it may be made to convey.

For instance, we might say, 'This writer declares his

meaning to be so and so; it is true his words may be brought to bear that *sense*, but such is not their obvious *import*.' Or again, 'The Articles of our Church have been received by certain writers in a non-natural *sense;* but whatever may have been the *meaning* of their compilers, the *import* is quite unlike what they are now made to say.'

AMUSEMENT, ENTERTAINMENT, DIVERSION, RECREATION.

These four words are sometimes used indifferently, but there are occasionally variations in their meaning.

'Diversion' often preserves something of its etymological sense, and conveys the idea of distracting the attention and drawing the mind from subjects fatiguing or depressing: at other times it is used to describe the lightest and gayest kind of pleasures, and those which excite most laughter and merriment. 'Recreation' adheres even more strictly to its etymology: it always implies refreshment after business or serious employment.* An idle person may enjoy amusement, entertainment, or diversion; but never recreation.

'Amusement' and 'entertainment' are perhaps the most alike in meaning; but there is this great difference, that a useful pursuit may be an amusement, if it pleases and recreates the mind: but nothing can be looked on in the light of 'entertainment' which is not pursued for sake of that alone. For instance, we should say, 'I find much *amusement* in gardening,' but not 'much *entertainment:*' or, 'I derive so much *amusement* from the labors of my garden, that I do not care for idle *diversions*.' Again, 'an entertainment' always conveys the idea of an elaborate show or spectacle, which is not given by 'an amusement,' or 'a diversion.' † 'Rec-

* See some Remarks on the subject in *English Life, Social and Domestic.*

* The conjugate adjective 'entertaining' is nearly the same as 'amusing.'

reation' differs from the other three in always implying that an active part is taken in it. We speak of 'the recreation of dancing,' but not 'the recreation of witnessing' a ballet: where the pleasure is *passive*, 'amusement' or 'entertainment is employed. We might express ourselves thus: 'They enjoyed the *recreation* of a game of cricket: the spectacle afforded much *amusement*, (or *entertainment*,) to the spectators: and the ludicrous falls of some of the players supplied them with infinite *diversion*.'

USAGE, CUSTOM.

'Whenever 'usage' is employed, 'custom' might be substituted, though with less force: but a custom is not necessarily a usage. A 'custom' is merely that which is often repeated; a 'usage' must be both often repeated and of long standing. Hence we may speak of 'a new custom,' but not of 'a new usage.'

The history of the word 'custom' is curious — it probably had the same origin as 'accost' — to come near — and thence 'to be habitual.' The root is the Latin 'costa,' the side or rib.

DEXTERITY, ADDRESS, SKILL.

'Dexterity' is most applicable to those actions in which there is more call for quickness and readiness with the hands than for deliberate contrivance and intelligence. 'Skill,' on the other hand, implies more of head and less of handwork. A cricket or billiard player shows *dexterity:* an artist or mechanician, *skill.* The same with the conjugate adjectives: a *dexterous* workman is quick, neat, and handy; a *skilful* workman understands the theory and practice of his business thoroughly: it would not be enough for a watchmaker to be dexterous, he must be also skilful.

'Address' is sometimes applied to feats of 'sleight of

hand,' but oftener to diplomatic readiness and acuteness in accommodating ourselves to those we have to deal with.

The French use 'address,' generally, where we use the word 'dexterity.'

HELP, AID, ASSISTANCE.

These words are nearly synonymous; but as generally happens when words of Saxon and Latin derivation are compared together, the Saxon word is the stronger. 'Help' implies more done by the helper, and less by the person helped, than 'aid' or 'assistance:' and it is the same with the conjugate verbs: we may *aid* a person in carrying a load, we *help* him out of a ditch into which he has fallen. Hence, in a religious sense, it is usual to speak of 'seeking help' not 'aid' from above, — unless we are understood to speak of a power *co-operating* with man; when the word 'aid' is admissible. In sudden distress the cry raised is always 'Help!' not 'aid.' In the common expressions, 'I cannot *help* this'—'you must *help* yourself,' the word 'aid' could not be substituted.*

'Assistance' implies still more of *co-operation*, and less of *succor*, than even 'aid.' Two persons are said to 'assist each other,' not 'to *aid* each other.' It implies *mutual* aid. We might say, 'Beaumont and Fletcher wrote plays, in which each afforded *assistance* to the other: Beaumont could not have succeeded without Fletcher's *aid*, and when he was in a difficulty his friend's *help* extricated him.'

ACT, ACTION, DEED.

These first two words are often synonymous, but there

---

* There is a curious colloquial incorrectness in the common phrase, 'Don't do so more than you *can help*:' correctly speaking, it should be 'more than you *can't* help;' though this last would sound so strange that it could hardly pass current.

are essential differences between them. 1st. — 'Act' does not necessarily imply an external result; 'action' always does. We may speak of repentance, for example, as an 'act:' we could not call it an 'action.' The expression, now nearly obsolete, but formerly common among Roman Catholic writers, and our older divines, of 'an *act* of faith, contrition, humility,' &c. — signifying merely a mental determination, — shows how strong was the tendency even then to extend the word 'act' to operations of the mind.*

2dly. — An act must be *individual:* we may speak of 'a course of action.' 'Action,' without the article, may even be spoken of in the abstract as opposed to a state of 'repose,' 'indolence,' or 'contemplation:' this could never be done with the word 'act.' †

Lastly. — 'Act,' when qualified, is oftener, though not universally, coupled with another substantive: 'action' always by an adjective preceding it. We speak of 'a kind action' — but of 'an *act of* kindness.' 'A kind act' might be admissible, though not usual; but 'an action of kindness' is an expression never used. Deed appears synonymous with 'act.'

ANGER, WRATH.

'Anger' is more correctly applied to the inward feeling: 'wrath' to the outward manifestation. Hence, in describing external effects, which *seem* like those produced by anger, the word 'wrath' is always used. We should not speak of

---

* The French use the expression '*actions* de grâces' for thanksgivings; this is evidently derived from the Latin, 'agere gratias.'

† The only way in which 'act' could be used without the article, would be in such an expression as 'in *act* to strike.'

the 'anger' but of the 'wrath' of the elements.* We therefore speak of 'the *wrath* of God,' more correctly than of his *anger*. We cannot attribute to Him passions like those of men: we can only describe the external effects which in men would be produced by those passions.

TYRANNY, DESPOTISM.

Both of these terms generally imply absolute power, and power which is exercised for the pleasure of the governor, not the benefit of the governed. But 'despotism' is applicable to a power which is regularly established by law, however unjustly: while 'tyranny' indicates the abuse of extensive power, whether legal or otherwise. A nation may be said either to suffer under 'despotism' or 'tyranny;' but the word 'despotism' draws attention to the absolute power of a government; 'tyranny,' to the severe and harsh use of that power. The word 'tyranny' is likewise much less limited to the description of the government of a *country*, than 'despotism.' We speak of the 'tyranny' exercised by a harsh parent or schoolmaster, or even by a stronger boy over a weaker. Even in an abstract sense, we often speak of 'the tyranny' of fashion, habit or the passions; in none of these cases could we use the word 'despotism.'†

Tyranny and despotism must both be unjust in all cases, since they imply a preference of the interest of the governor to that of the governed: but a tyranny must also necessarily be cruel: a despotism may be mild, and even in its way beneficent. A slave-owner may be benevolent and

---

* See Scott's *Rokeby*:

> 'Mine be the eve of tropic sun!
> No pale gradations mark his way,
> No twilight dews his *wrath* allay.'

† The conjugate adjective, 'despotic,' somewhat differs from the substantive in this respect. We do speak of 'a despotic parent,' &c

kind to his serfs, but his government of them must be a despotism, that being implied in the very meaning of the word, which has deviated but little from its original etymological signification in Greek : —'a master of slaves' (*Despotes*).

Tyranny, on the contrary, originally implied merely an absolute government. It is used in this sense by the early Greek poets: though the oldest *prose* writers on record apply the word exclusively to those who had *usurped* absolute power in a free country.

It is a curious satire on human nature, that the word which originally implied only unlimited power, should have afterwards come to imply the *abuse* of that power, as if the last was the necessary consequence of the first.*

LIBERTY, FREEDOM.

When applied to the *condition* either of a nation or individual, these words are strictly synonymous, and conjugates of the same adjective 'free;' but when used in ordinary polite conversation, there is the same shade of difference which is observable (as has been remarked before) in other pairs of Saxon and Latin synonymes. 'May I take the liberty?' is an expression in frequent use : 'may I take the *freedom*?' would be considered as a piece of vulgarism.

VESTIGES, TRACES.

These words have a corresponding origin, and are often synonymous; when they differ, the word 'vestiges' is always applied in its analogical sense, while 'traces' may be used either in this or in its primary sense. We follow the

---

* It has been suggested that the Greek *Tyrannos* may be nearly related to the Irish Tigernach (pronounced Tierna) a chief or lord, which is the word used as an equivalent to *Kurios* in the Greek Testament.

traces of a person or animal lost sight of: we discover the *vestiges* of earlier formations in geology. In this last sense the word 'traces' might be equally well used: but we never speak of 'the vestiges of foot-marks in a wood,' &c.

It may be observed that words of Latin origin are much sooner corrupted from their original signification than Anglo-Saxon ones: probably from the *body* of the language being essentially Teutonic.

CHASTISEMENT, PUNISHMENT, PENALTY.

According to its primary sense, 'punishment' meant neither more nor less than vengeance or retribution. It originally implied the giving *satisfaction* to individuals: hence the Latin expression '*sumere pœnas*,' (to *take* or receive the punisment of an offender); and '*luere* [or *solvere*] *pœnas*' (to 'pay,' or discharge the penalty). In short, punishment was correlative to the sentiment of *anger;* and accordingly Bacon speaks of revenge as 'a wild justice.' But in its established modern sense, both punishment and chastisement may be defined as pain inflicted with a view to *prevent* future wrong-doing. The chief difference between them is, that 'punishment' is the term applied to designate suffering inflicted with a view to deter either the sufferer or others: while 'chastisement' is confined to the individual who is the object of it, and is supposed and intended to have some reforming and corrective, as well as deterring power.

Hence afflictions are called the 'chastisements' (not the *punishments*) sent by Providence: but the future retribution of the wicked is spoken of as a 'punishment,' because it cannot act as a corrective, but as a terror (in prospect) to offenders.

The pains inflicted by the law of the land are, correctly speaking, punishments, not chastisements; for though some of them may happen to be of a reformatory character, their *primary* object is to deter, not to correct.

A 'penalty' is a punishment considered in the light of a debt incurred by certain offences, which must be *paid off* by its object. The expression, when used in reference to the law, is oftenest applied to fines; and in a more general application it is used to describe those sufferings which are the *natural consequences* of a fault, and which may be considered as the debt which the offender incurs. We should say, 'sickness, or poverty, is the *penalty* which the intemperate, or the extravagant, must pay for their criminal indulgences.'

PROJECT, DESIGN, SCHEME, PLAN.

All these words imply a certain end in view, and means used to accomplish it: of the four, 'design' looks most to the end, and least to the means: 'scheme' and 'plan' most to the means and least to the end: while 'project' seems to hold a middle place between the extremes.

'Scheme,' in accordance with its original root (*schema*, a pattern), implies something fully formed and sketched out. 'Plan' conveys this idea even more fully, and betokens a more advanced and matured state than 'scheme.'

For instance: 'they formed a *project* to revolutionize the country: with this *design* they concocted a *scheme;* they then met together to mature their *plan.*'

PURPOSE, INTENT, INTENTION.

The word 'purpose' always implies the use of some means towards an end; with 'intention' this is not the case. For instance, 'he had long harbored the *intention* of taking the life of his enemy, and for this *purpose* he provided himself with weapons.'

'Purpose' has some resemblance to 'design.' (See the

head, *Design, project, scheme:*) It was originally a corruption of 'pro-pose,' and the conjugate of the verb 'to propose,' or 'to purpose,' as it was formerly called.

'Intent' and 'intention' are much the same in signification. 'Intent' was used in old English where 'intention' would now be employed; (as may be seen from the technical expression, 'with *intent* to kill.' 'Intention' was *then* never used except—

First, in the logical sense of 'first or second intentions.'

Secondly, in a technical theological sense,* which it still preserves: *i. e.* the Romish doctrine of intention, which inculcates that if a priest administers any of the sacraments without the inward will and determination to exercise his priestly function, those sacraments are null and void.

[See the *Archives of the Council of Trent*, where an anathema is pronounced upon those who doubt the truth of this doctrine. See also some remarks on the subject in the third number of the *Cautions for the Times.*]

LIST, CATALOGUE.

A catalogue always implies some description of the articles named; a list, though it does not *exclude* a description, only *implies* a simple enumeration. Hence, we never speak of a catalogue of subscribers, a visiting catalogue, &c., because then the names alone are enumerated: but the contents of a museum, library, or picture gallery, are said to be set down in a 'catalogue,' because something *answering* to a description is always appended, though it may only be the title of a book, which is not a mere arbitrary sound like the name of an individual, but conveys some sort of description of its contents.

---

* Many of the old technical terms in theology were scarcely altered from the Latin.

BREVITY, CONCISENESS.

'Brevity' is often used indifferently with 'conciseness;' but when any difference is implied, then properly speaking, 'brevity' refers to the matter, and 'conciseness' to the style. In fact, when brevity of *style* is spoken of, it may be considered as synonymous with 'conciseness.' Strictly speaking, however, 'brevity' merely implies the use of few words, while 'conciseness' implies a great deal of matter concentrated in a small space.

Brevity is sometimes attained by leaving much unsaid: in such a case, what *is* said is not necessarily expressed with conciseness;* this last can only be attained by long practice in the art of compressing.

A concise discourse is like a well-packed trunk, which contains much more than it at first sight appears to do: a brief discourse *may* be like a trunk half full; short, because it is scanty.

TOLERANCE, TOLERATION.

Tolerance is a habit of mind; toleration applies to action, not disposition. Principles of *tolerance* will lead to the *toleration* of different opinions.

CONFIDENCE, TRUST, RELIANCE.

Confidence implies trust — but trust does not always imply confidence. *Trust* is rather particular than general: we may feel trust in a man's honesty, but not in his good judgment, &c.; but confidence, though sometimes used in this partial sense, is also used in reference to the general character. But we may repose trust in a person in whose character, as a whole, we have no confidence. For instance,

---

* See *Midsummer Night's Dream* — 'A tedious brief play.'

we might say, 'I can *trust** in such a person's acting in this way because it is his interest, or, he is afraid of acting otherwise;' these expressions themselves imply that the person referred to is unworthy of *confidence.* 'Reliance' is only applied to qualities or actions: not in general to persons; if so used, it may usually be considered as transferred by metonymy from the action or quality to the person qualified.

ERROR, MISTAKE, BLUNDER.

'Error' is always used to designate some action which is *blamed*, whether morally or intellectually. It may proceed from nothing but a failure in judgment; still the word implies some degree of blame, though generally slight. An error is always a mistake; a mistake is not always an error. A mistake *may* attach no sort of blame to the person who makes it; it may even be 'a *fortunate* mistake.'

A blunder implies a mistake which is inconsistent with the *knowledge the agent possesses.* If any one is said to make a blunder in spelling or grammar, it implies that he is acquainted with both. We talk, it is true, of 'blundering on an object in the dark,' but this is rather for want of a more correct expression.

A 'bull' is in fact a blunder.

MALICE, SPITE.

These words are often used indifferently, and both imply a desire of giving pain for its own sake; but there are important distinctions between them.

Malice, like its conjugate 'malicious,' is applied not only to individual acts, but to the whole character and disposition; 'spite' and 'spiteful,' only to individual manifesta-

* The verbs and nouns correspond exactly.

tions. For when a person is described as 'spiteful,' it is always with reference to some particular speech or action. Malice, as its root (*malum*) would seem to imply, is often used to describe an utterly unprovoked and spontaneous desire of giving pain: in French, it is used to express a mere love of teasing for fun's sake; in English, it describes that ill-will which often springs originally from that principle when perverted and exaggerated.

'Spite,' which *immediately* is derived from *despite* (dépit), seems traceable to the Latin root *despuo*, to spit out, as if something loathsome and offensive. It has still preserved so much of its etymology, as to imply ill-will resulting from some feeling of pique, anger, or opposition; and it generally indicates a low and petty manifestation of the feeling. A cruel boy will torment a younger child or an animal from malice; a successful candidate is slandered by his rivals from spite.

OCCUPATION, BUSINESS, AVOCATION.

The word 'occupation' is applied to whatever employs us, either at the moment or habitually. 'Business' must always be a necessary, or, at least, important and pressing occupation — something connected with our profession or other duties in life; while 'occupation' may describe a merely amusing or ornamental pursuit. Painting affords an agreeable *occupation* to an amateur; to a professional artist it is a *business*.

An 'avocation,' strictly speaking, is, as its root (*a*-voco) indicates, that which calls us off, hinders us, from other employments. It can, therefore, be only correctly used relatively to other things.

NOVEL, ROMANCE.

Both these words have widely diverged from their etymology. Originally a *novel* meant merely a *new tale.** *Now* (as the common term, 'a *new* novel,' may show) the idea of newness is nowise connected with it. To define a novel is no very easy task; but it generally seems to convey the idea of something longer and more elaborate than a mere 'tale;' and the complement of three volumes appears even more closely connected with it than the magic 'five acts' with a tragedy.

A *romance* originally meant something written in the *Romance* language, the old *langue d'oc* of the south of France, which was the vehicle of the earliest poety of the middle ages. Thence it has now come to signify a tale of a wild, high-flown, adventurous, and poetical cast — something very far removed from ordinary life.

The French have also preserved the word 'romance,' but use it to describe a very different style of composition — the lyrical ballad. 'Roman' seems to apply equally to the novel and the 'romance.'

POVERTY, INDIGENCE, PAUPERISM.

Poverty simply implies a difficulty in supporting oneself in one's own station; it is therefore relative; what is poverty to a gentleman would be affluence to a laborer.

Indigence implies extreme distress, and almost destitution.

Pauperism signifies being maintained in idleness by public charity; it is therefore the most hopelessly degrading state of all. A poor man, even an indigent man, may retain his independence of character and self-respect: but a pauper is degraded in his own eyes and those of all others. En-

* In old English, a 'novelist' signified a propounder of *new opinions* in science or politics.

couraged, nay, urged on, to a life of indolent inaction, and owing his wretched subsistence to that *forced* charity which, reversing the description of 'the quality of *mercy*,' which '*is not strained*' — may be said truly, to be 'doubly *cursed* — cursing him that gives and him that takes' — his existence cannot but be miserable and degraded.

MATTER, SUBJECT.

The matter of a discourse, book, &c., is from within; the subject, from without. The matter comprises the arguments used and the substance of what is said — all, in short, except what concerns the *style* of writing or speaking.

The subject, on the other hand, is the theme of the discourse, that *about which* the arguments are brought forward.

Two persons taking different sides in a debate must treat of the same *subject:* but the *matter* of their discourse must be different.

We might say — 'The *subject* of discussion was very interesting: in Mr. A.'s speech the *matter* was good, though ill-expressed; Mr. B.'s style was better, but his *matter* inferior.'

LANGUAGE, WORDS, TERMS, EXPRESSIONS.

In classing these substantives together, we do not, of course, allude to their separate and independent meanings, but merely to the sense in which they are used to describe the matter and manner of a discourse. 'Words' are used to designate the simple meaning and sense of what is said, without any allusion to its manner, style, or grammatical accuracy. 'Language,' on the other hand, is generally used to describe these latter characteristics. If we praise any one for using 'good language,' we are understood to praise his correctness of style and manner, not his matter; but if we say, 'These are *good words*,' this, though not a usual expression, would be understood to refer to the *meaning* of what was said. The phrase 'bitter words,' would be used to describe words whose *meaning* was bitter.

'Terms' are generally used to describe or define something else: and one *term* may be composed of several *words*.

'Expressions' resemble 'language,' but apply more to individual words or phrases, and less to the general tenor of a discourse.

'Words,' 'terms,' and 'language' may sometimes be used indifferently — as when we speak of 'delivering an opinion in plain *terms*, *words*, or *language;* in such a phrase as this, 'expressions' would be inadmissible.

SUGGESTION, HINT.

A *suggestion* is generally supposed to furnish us with some *practical* assistance or directions; a *hint* implies something slighter and more covert, and may be merely negative in its tendency.

We may throw out a 'hint' against some one's character — we dissuade another from taking certain steps by a timely 'hint:' in neither of these cases could we be said to give a 'suggestion.'

We might say — 'He gave me a *hint* of the danger to which I was exposed; and afterwards supplied me with *suggestions* as to the best means of avoiding it.'

MOMENT, INSTANT.

These words are most commonly synonymous; where they differ, 'instant' seems to imply something even more speedy than 'moment.' 'This instant,' conveys the idea of greater rapidity than 'this moment.' Another difference may be mentioned; the expression, 'a few moments'—'two or three moments'—is not uncommon: 'a few instants' is never used. In this, our habit of speaking presents a striking contrast to the French, with whom 'quelques instants' is such a favorite expression

INDEX.

THE END.

www.ingramcontent.com/pod-product-compliance
Lightning Source LLC
LaVergne TN
LVHW011230110826
845150LV00006B/1592

* 9 7 8 1 4 2 5 5 1 4 4 6 4 *